GIVE ME
FREEDOM

GIVE ME
FREEDOM

by May McNeer,
Drawings by Lynd Ward

New York   ABINGDON PRESS   *Nashville*

CONTENTS

To Freedom's Shore

WILLIAM PENN

A wintry English wind nipped the nose of five-year-old William Penn, riding to school perched on the saddle in front of the groom. The day was January 30, 1649. The groom was as pale and silent as Dame Margaret Penn had been when she kissed Will goodbye at the door of their home in Wanstead. To Will the steady clopping of the horse's hooves on frozen mud of the road was like the sound of minutes ticking off time. In Chigwell Village he was placed down on the road. He walked slowly into his school and approached a group of his friends.

"When—when will he . . ."

"Listen. Listen for the bells. You'll know. But what do we care? We are all against the king. He tried to dissolve Parliament, didn't he? He's a Catholic, isn't he? We're all Protestants."

Will saw that this older boy, in spite of his loud words, was as pale and frightened as they all were, even their Puritan schoolmaster. Will knew that his father, young Admiral William Penn, although an officer of great distinction, was a Protestant. On his father's last visit home he had heard his parents talking about the crisis in the government.

"The king is a good man, but he wants to rule without

Parliament. And he rules England badly, forcing the country into debt and great poverty."

"Yes. Feeling against the king is strong, and it is spreading. There are those in Parliament—and in the army—who wish to go slowly, but there are others who would go too far."

This day in 1649 violent members of Parliament were going too far. The whole schoolroom was tense and Will felt a suffocating fear. He waited for the tolling bells that would signal the beheading of King Charles I. All England seemed to hold its breath with him as he listened. Village bells began to ring, echoing the many deep-throated bells of London thirteen miles away. Their schoolmaster was praying, simply and earnestly, and the boys bowed their heads too.

When the bells were silent Will knew that England had passed out of the reign of the Catholic royal house of England and into the rule of Protestants, who controlled the army and Parliament. They would form a commonwealth under Oliver Cromwell, known as "Ironsides" because of the armor he wore and the kind of man he was. Cromwell, who was both a military and political leader of great force, became "Protector" of England.

During the next few years Will Penn came to understand that although there were good things done by Cromwell, persecution of innocent persons was still widespread in England. Now instead of the persecution of Puritans, many of whom had been forced to flee to America under royal rule, there was persecution of Catholics. The despised Quakers were hounded by both Catholics and Protestants. There was still no freedom to worship in the British Isles, and there was no peace.

William Penn was a tall, strong boy whose mischief

10

in school sometimes brought his teacher to call on William's mother, Dame Margaret. Shaking his weary head the schoolmaster said, "He is restless and mighty lively in the classroom, mighty lively, ma'am. I wish he could feel the stinging end of a stick from his father for my caning seems not enough."

"You know, sir, that my husband is seldom at home. Commanding the fleet for Cromwell keeps him on the high seas. Our two boys can scarcely recall his face, let alone the end of his cane. I will talk to Will and try to bring him to more thoughtful ways."

Dame Margaret spoke sternly to her older son, and yet she could not keep a twinkle from her eyes. She had a strong and lively nature too. And well did she need strength and independence to manage her household alone so much of the time.

When William was thirteen he went with his mother to London to live in lodgings near the ancient Tower in the same neighborhood in which he had been born. This was not a happy return to London for the Penns. Will's brother had died, and his father was in serious trouble. The Protector had given honors as well as a valuable estate in Ireland to Admiral Penn in gratitude for his service to the Commonwealth. Then Cromwell had received a secret report that his admiral was part of a group plotting to bring the son of the beheaded king to the throne from exile in France. The Protector had ordered the admiral's arrest and imprisonment in the Tower of London.

Day after day Will watched his mother's face become drawn with anxiety as she visited members of Cromwell's government trying to get help for her husband. William grew sad and thoughtful himself as he waited in their little rooms or strolled to the docks to sniff salt air and tarry ropes and to watch the ships come in.

When the admiral was released he was made to promise that he would leave England and live on his estate in Ireland. Will was glad to be in the country on the beautiful Macroom estate near the town of Cork. He had horses to ride and green hills to roam, and sometimes he walked alone about the narrow streets of Cork. His father and mother visited with the landed gentry and entertained their wealthy neighbors. Many of them were English, but they were all strangers to the ways and the thinking of the poor people who had not much more than potatoes to eat.

At fifteen Will was already different from his parents. He became acquainted with townsfolks in shops and farmers living in thatched cottages. One misty afternoon he stepped into a small room where a service was being held. Sitting down near the door, Will listened to the strong but quiet voice of Thomas Loe. Loe was a hosier, a seller of stockings, in Oxford, England. He was also a member of the Society of Friends, called Quakers,

and he often went on journeys to speak for the little religious group. Will heard a talk such as he had never listened to before. He came away with some new thoughts.

Not long after that day Will was sent to London to prepare for entrance to Oxford University. He lived on Tower Hill again and studied under a tutor.

Although fighting had broken out once more in England, it was quiet enough on Tower Hill. Yet William Penn knew that important changes were coming soon to the country. Oliver Cromwell had died in 1858, and his weak son Richard had soon resigned the office of Protector of England. Will realized that his father would welcome and take part in a movement to bring the prince back from exile, and place him on the English throne as Charles II.

William was sixteen in 1660 when, to the great delight of his father, he was admitted to Oxford University. Admiral Penn, now Admiral Sir William Penn, had special plans for the future of his only son. William would inherit estates and a comfortable fortune some day, and he must prepare to fill an important position in the royal court. Will had grown up sharing his father's belief in royalty, and he expected to lead the life arranged for him.

The day on which Charles II entered his kingdom was marked with brilliant pomp and ceremony in London. William joined his mother and friends at a window to watch his father riding in the long procession of courtiers. Buildings were hung with silken banners and flowers were spread in the streets for the king's carriage to roll over. Bells clanged joyously, echoed and re-echoed from tower to tower until the city and countryside was a concert of jubilant sound. In the midst of his own shouting William remembered quite suddenly the slow tolling of great bells that day eleven years before. He fell silent, wondering what this new king would bring to England. When he returned to college he went again to the Quaker meeting to hear Thomas Loe.

At Oxford that year William heard disturbing things. Although Charles had declared he would maintain religious tolerance, supporters of the king were persecuting professors for Puritan beliefs. William joined a group of students banded together to protect these teachers. On several occasions he and his friends jumped on Catholic students who were disturbing professors and tore their academic gowns from their shoulders. These actions aroused the authorities and William Penn and his friends were dismissed from the university.

The admiral's face grew almost purple when he heard of it.

"William," he roared, "have I not provided you with money and position? Have I not made it easy for you to have one of

the highest offices in court? Yet you behave like one of those demented Quakers."

The elder Penn rose from his chair, grasped a whip from the wall, and beat his son unmercifully. William stood quietly under the blows. He said nothing to defend himself, although he was not yet a Quaker. He simply believed that everyone should be allowed to worship as he pleased. At last his father threw down the whip and ordered his son from the house.

A short time later Dame Margaret persuaded her husband to permit their son to return home. The admiral did so only because Will promised to go to Europe to study for two years. When he left for Paris with several young lords he almost believed that his father had been right that the queer beliefs of Quakers were not for him.

Admiral Penn, gouty foot propped on a stool at home, pounded his fist joyfully when he learned that William was not only studying at the College of Saumur but was also going to court balls. The admiral was even more pleased when he heard that his son had won a duel with a drunken lord in the street, and had spared the courtier his life. At last William was becoming a "gentleman" in the eyes of his father.

At nineteen Will enjoyed wearing a powdered wig under his plumed hat. Smallpox had thinned his brown hair as a child, and ever since he had felt ashamed of his looks. From that time he always wore a wig, although it was not always a powdered one. When he returned to London his father's friend, Samuel Pepys, writer of a famous diary of the times, said of William, "I perceive something of learning he has got, but a great deal, if not too much, of the vanity of the French garb and affected manner of speech and gait."

Back in London William decided to study law. He was still a dandy in his dress, and his companions were wild and spendthrift sons of lords. He roamed the streets with them at night, fighting thieving footpads, and roistering nobility as well.

In the midst of his gaiety, William received a letter from his father directing him to come at once to the flagship. The admiral wanted his son on his naval staff for a time. War was being waged with Holland and the British fleet was assembling for battle on the sea. Admiral Penn thought it time his son had a taste of gunfire.

William arrived on the ship looking like a dandy, but he did not remain one for long. He displayed such astonishing courage under fire that the admiral pounded him on the back and roared out his pride and approval.

The Duke of York, brother of the king, was commander of the navy. He was aboard the flagship for a part of William's service. William came to know and respect him and was especially happy when the duke commanded him to take an urgent dispatch to the king.

William left the ship at Harwich and flung himself on a horse. Riding furiously through rain and mud he pounded along the rough road to London. Covered with mud he arrived in the palace before the sovereign was out of bed. William, who had expected to deliver the dispatch to a courtier, was amazed to see King Charles himself striding in his sleeping robe to take the message in person.

His father, having decided that his son had seen enough of the navy to prove himself, now allowed William to return to his law studies and his gay friends. The hot, dry summer of 1665 was followed by an unusually severe winter. Many people took to their beds with a sickness known as the black plague, and few ever got up again. The disease spread rapidly through the dark and dirty city of London. None knew where it had come from, but some believed that rats brought it ashore from ships tied up in the Thames.

Panic ran with the disease, until all of the rich left the city as fast as horses and coaches could carry them. There was no more roistering in the crooked, silent streets. After awhile William could hear nothing but the rumble of carts carrying away the dead. He took to wearing sober clothing and a short brown wig.

His thoughts were sober too. He began to think again of religion—of the questions of life and death. Slowly he returned to his Quaker beliefs. When his father ordered him to Ireland to manage the estate, he went reluctantly. For a short time he became an officer in an Irish army regiment, but he did not like fighting Irish rebels. In Cork he heard Thomas Loe preach again,

and he reached a decision that was to change his whole future. He went to Loe and said that he wished to become a member of the Society of Friends.

Quakers believed in peace, although a Quaker did not live a peaceful life. William Penn was arrested very soon after he began to preach in Cork.

His interview with his angry father afterwards was far more disturbing than the jail had been. Feeling that he would be better off out of Ireland, William had gone to England where he began to put his religious views into pamphlets. The admiral sent for him. "Why are you doing this? And take off your hat to your father!"

His son, standing before him in gray Quaker clothing and a wide-brimmed hat, replied quietly, "Sir, I honor my father, but I believe with the Friends that a man should bare his head only to God."

William Penn was no sooner in London than he was taken off to jail again for attending a Quaker meeting. He sat in the Tower, completing his stirring pamphlets on freedom of

religion. His prison was near the Church of Allhallows Barking, where he had been baptized in the Church of England faith. Among the dark shadows of the Tower where Anne Boleyn, once queen to Henry the Eighth, and Mary, Queen of Scots, had spent their last hours, William Penn wrote his famous *No Cross, No Crown*. He had no books to refer to. From his remarkable memory he put down the beliefs of many great men who had written on life, death, and man's responsibility to his fellow men.

"Old Penn," as the retired admiral now was called, sent a friend to tell his son that he would get him out of the Tower if he would give up his Quaker beliefs.

William replied, "Thou may tell my father that my prison shall be my grave before I budge a jot. I owe my conscience to no mortal man."

Nevertheless "Old Penn" did ask his friend the Duke of York to have William released and to offer him a place as ambassador. This offer William refused, standing again before the admiral, once more, hat on head. His father turned nearly purple again, as he shouted, "You may 'thee' and 'thou' whomsoever you please except the king, the Duke of York, and myself. And take off your hat in respect to me." This his Quaker son would not do.

Finding the bailiffs had closed a meeting house, Penn and a fellow missionary preached in the street. They were promptly arrested. The trial that followed became a milestone in English law. In a courtroom crowded with a noisy throng eating oranges and bread, William Penn conducted his own defense before twelve judges and a jury. When the judges saw he was convincing·the jury they had him lowered into a well, or hole, built into the floor at the back of the courtroom. In this deep well the prisoner could hear but could not be heard. William Penn was determined to be heard.

He kept leaping up and hauling himself above the top, shouting in his loud, deep voice. Every time that a guard hit his hands, he fell back, then up he jumped again!

The jury brought in a verdict of "Not guilty." The two Quakers were innocent of the charge of preaching to an "unlawful, seditious, and riotous assembly." The judges were so angry that they fined both the jury and the defendants forty marks each. When all of them refused to pay they were thrown in jail. While the jury and the Quakers sat in prison the case was appealed to a higher court. There the sentence was reversed and the fines removed. This case settled in law the rights of a jury as well as of prisoners, and it established the freedom of all English citizens on a firmer basis than ever before.

William Penn was soon called to the deathbed of his father who, in his last days, seemed to understand his son better. He murmured, "Son William, live all in love, shun evil, and I pray God to bless you."

At the age of twenty-six William was heir to several estates and a small fortune. On a fine day in April he visited a Quaker friend in the country. In a cottage nearby lived the blind poet, John Milton, author of "Paradise Lost." There William met Gulielma Springett, a lovely young Quaker girl who was a friend of Milton's daughter. Two years later William Penn and Gulielma were married and went to live on a small estate outside of London.

Many happy years with Guli and their six children did not change Penn's devotion to the defense of the despised Quakers. He recalled the old friendship held by King Charles and the Duke of York, for the elder Penn, and he went to them to ask for the release of Quaker prisoners. The royal brothers laughed at stubborn Will Penn, who still refused to remove his Quaker hat before them, yet they respected him for his courage.

For some time Penn had been interested in America and the growing colonies in the New World. Now he began to think of that wild land as a refuge for persecuted Quakers. King Charles still owed money to William's father's estate for the admiral had made a loan to the king while he was in exile in France. Will, the Quaker, asked the king for a large tract of land in America in payment of this debt. He received it. With the help of friends, Penn drew up a constitution for his colony. In it he asserted that "liberty without obedience is confusion, and obedience without liberty is slavery."

In October of the year 1682, William Penn arrived on the shore of the Delaware River with a hundred Quaker settlers. He named his land Pennsylvania in honor of his father. Shiploads of Quakers came to settle the town of Philadelphia and to call it the "City of Brotherly Love." More arrivals pushed out into the

forests to clear the land and make farms in the wilderness.

William Penn believed it of utmost importance to be friendly and fair with the Indians of that region. He wished to pay them for the loss of their hunting grounds. Penn had a talent for languages, and it wasn't long before he was speaking to the Delaware Indians in their own tongue. He rode his big white horse into their villages, where they received him with the honors accorded a chief.

Sometimes Mr. Penn laid his hat aside, along with his gray coat, and joined in the games of the braves. A loud shout of admiration rose as he leaped farther than any other. The Indians knew they were always welcome at Penn's home in Philadelphia, where feasts of meats, buckwheat cakes, and cornbread would be spread for them.

Under a tall oak at Shackamaxon, beside the river, William Penn met the Delawares to sign a treaty. Facing the

chieftains in their buckskins, paint, and feathers, the Quaker stood in a suit of fine gray cloth, with a sky-blue sash about his waist, and his wide-brimmed hat on his head. He spoke to them in their own language with such dignity and eloquence that his words were remembered and repeated through the years to generations of tribal children. The treaty they signed promised faith and friendship in the settling of differences. The Delawares never shed a drop of Quaker blood until after Penn's death, and then only because a white man murdered an Indian and broke the solemn pact of friendship.

Roger Williams had already settled Rhode Island as a refuge for religious dissenters before Penn came to America. Yet it was William Penn who established a colony with the strongest guarantees of religious freedom for all.

After a few years Penn returned to England, where he tried to protect all Protestant faiths, as well as the Quaker. Penn used his friendship with the Catholic King James, formerly the Duke of York, to intervene for all Protestants, but his Protestant friends, and even the Quakers, came to distrust Penn because he was always welcomed at court. When James was overthrown and the reign of the Protestants William and Mary began William Penn was no longer invited to court.

He led a lonely life on his estate. Guli died, and his sadness was increased by the fact that only two of his children still lived. His son was a wild youth, causing Penn much concern and unhappiness.

A few years later William Penn married a young girl, Hannah Callowhill, and they sailed for the colony in America. A son, John, was born to William and Hannah. Penn had built a manor house twenty miles upriver from Philadelphia. His large home filled rapidly with more children until his second family numbered seven.

After a while Penn, who loved his colony, agreed to return to England to please his wife. When his health failed he turned the colony over to the English crown and received a small payment for the fortune he had put into it. The only promise he asked of Queen Mary was that she take the Quakers under her protection.

William Penn died in 1718. His Pennsylvania colony, founded on the principles of religious freedom, was his great gift to America.

Voice of the Revolution

THOMAS PAINE

Just one hundred and one years after William Penn had listened to deep-throated bells tolling for the beheading of a king, another boy squirmed on an English schoolroom bench.

This was in a Quaker school in the village of Thetford, Norfolkshire, England. Thirteen-year-old Tom Paine felt as trapped as the blue bottle fly buzzing and banging hopelessly against a grimy window. He lowered his head and sat quietly as stern Master Knowles fixed suspicious eyes on him. Although Quakers believed in peace and friendly persuasion, Master Knowles did not practice these virtues. He was as cruel as all the other schoolmasters of the time. Tom looked on him with contempt mixed with fear, remembering punishments for noisiness or lack of study in reading, writing and mathematics.

His teacher did not know how well Tom could read in English, which was the language taught in the school. Latin and Greek were not taught to lower class boys in 1750. Tom found it hard to remain quiet for long, yet when the schoolmaster talked of his youth as a chaplain on a man-o'-war Tom sat still, his keen, intent blue eyes fixed on the speaker. Tom spent a good deal of time figuring out ways of leading the master into telling of these exciting experiences and he often succeeded in doing so.

From the street outside there came to Tom's ears a constant sound of horses' hooves on the cobbles of the village square. From the jail next door to the school there came the cries and curses of prisoners being whipped. After school, as the boys ran home in twilight, Tom tried not to look at a grim shape swinging on the gallows before the jail, or to remember that this man was hanged for speaking against the king. He also avoided the stocks and the pillory, filled with half-dead wretches suffering punishment for small offenses. He dashed as fast as his strong legs could carry him to his own cottage.

Thomas Paine was the son of a Quaker corsetmaker as stern and strict as Master Knowles. His father was waiting when Tom came into the bare little home. His mother glanced at him anxiously as his father said, "Another complaint from Master Knowles, Thomas. Thee are a great size now, as big as I am. I have told the schoolmaster that I will take thee out of school this time and put thee into my business as a full-time apprentice."

Tom scowled furiously. He hated making corsets for stout women and dandified men. He said nothing, but he decided that he would wait no longer to run away and ship out as a cabin boy on a man-o'-war in His Majesty's fleet.

The night was dark, but Tom had no trouble in slipping out of the cottage and finding the road to the sea. When he came to the harbor, weary from tramping the highway and sleeping in hedgerows, he stared in dismay at the name that he saw on the bow of a privateer vessel tied up at the dock. It was the "Terrible."

A sailor spat on the ground and grinned, "Know the name of the captain of the 'Terrible'? It's Captain Death!"

Tom gasped and turned to run—and then he thought of the hated corset shop. He would go to sea, but not with Captain Death. After awhile he found a ship called the "Vengeance" and was taken on as cabin boy. As he was waiting to go aboard he heard a horse pulled up behind him. His father, looking both stern and sorrowful, dismounted and approached.

"Boy, thee cannot do this thing. These ships make war, and thee has been taught differently. They will beat and starve thee aboard too. Come home!"

Tom thought of his mother's patient face and sad eyes, and, truth to tell, he was already a bit homesick. He went back to the corset shop, jogging along behind his father on the old horse.

As the days passed he hated the job as much as ever, although he was quick to learn the trade. His fingers were nimble to do the bidding of his mind, which was as sharp as the long needle that he used.

As dull days lengthened into dreary weeks and months, Tom grew desperate again. Again he ran away. This time he sailed on a privateer named the "King of Prussia." He found life at sea far from dull but no better than his father had said. After months of beatings and hunger for Tom, the ship docked in London. Tom slipped ashore, never to sign up again. He would not go home however. For awhile he was an apprentice to a shoemaker, and then to several other tradesmen. When he was sixteen he had gone back to the work that he knew best. He became a journeyman, or traveling, corsetmaker.

By the time he was twenty-two Tom was making stays, as corsets were often called, in the town of Sandwich. There he met Mary, a lively servant girl, who married him and helped set up a corsetmaking shop. The shop failed, and Tom and Mary then moved from one town to another, unable to make a living.

After a few years his wife died and Thomas Paine took a job as exciseman, or tax collector. He traveled about on horseback and was often in danger, for this job required collecting taxes from tavern keepers and rum smugglers. He got mighty little pay for doing it, too.

While Tom was rooming for awhile in the home of a tobacco merchant's widow he fell in love with her daughter, and soon married her. This marriage was unhappy, and so after a few months Tom Paine moved away. He was an angry man—angry at the way life had treated him and angry at the poverty and crime

that he saw all about him. He began to put his thoughts into writing. This was not as difficult as he had expected, for his hunger for knowledge had caused him since boyhood to read every book, pamphlet, or paper that he could find. He published a pamphlet telling of the hard lives of tax collectors, whose wages could not be raised without an act of Parliament. Although his pamphlet was widely read, nothing was done to improve the conditions that he was so unhappy about.

Tom decided there was no future for him in England, and he would go to America. When he heard that Benjamin

Franklin, a statesman from the American colonies, was visiting London he went to the place where Mr. Franklin was staying. Holding his pamphlet in one hand Paine pulled furiously on the doorbell with the other. If Mr. Franklin refused to see him he was prepared to force his way in. Paine had never had any reason to put trust in people who were in high positions. He believed that he had to fight his way upward in life.

The door opened. "Yes, sir?" said a quiet servant.

Paine's eyes burned. He placed a hand on the half open door, expecting refusal. "I came to see Mr. Franklin. My name is Thomas Paine."

"Come in, sir. Will you wait here?"

Before he could collect his thoughts Tom Paine, the poor tax collector, was shown into a room where a portly gentleman with mild eyes behind gold-rimmed spectacles was sitting at a writing desk.

"Be seated, Mr. Paine. What can I do for you?"

Tom's astonishment changed to eagerness as he told Mr. Franklin who he was and that he wished to go to America. He was even more surprised when Benjamin Franklin gave him a letter to his son-in-law in Philadelphia and took Paine's pamphlet with a promise to read it.

The voyage to America was long and rough. Tom Paine was so ill that when he went ashore in Philadelphia he was thin and gaunt. Mr. Franklin's son-in-law was pleasant but not of much help. He suggested that Tom become a "shilling schoolmaster" to the children of some of his friends. Tom made scarcely enough money at this to pay for food and a room in one of the many rows of small houses on a Philadelphia street.

32

His only amusement was strolling through the town and looking at the crowd. Quakers in sober gray rubbed shoulders with Indians in buckskin, whose brown skins and lithe walk looked strange to Tom's English eyes. He saw wealthy farmers and merchants followed by Negro slaves or white servants who had been sold to the colonists to pay for debts in the old country. Now and then he paused to listen to the talk of wild-looking trappers and frontiersmen who told of deep forests and distant rivers in this still largely unknown and unexplored land.

Tom Paine's other interest was reading. He was always hungry for knowledge, and he was rapidly educating himself. After awhile he found a chance to write. He went to work for a Scottish printer named Aitken, who gave him the job of writing and editing *The Pennsylvania Magazine*. Tom still made only a small wage, but he liked this work very much. His writing was clear, informed, and lively. The paper was so good that it soon was widely read.

Editor Paine, still wearing shabby clothing, came to know many prominent men of the colonies—George Washington, Thomas Jefferson, Samuel Adams, and others. Paine could talk of England to them, and they could tell him of the colonists' rising resentment at the unjust treatment that they received from their king and country. Colonists had to pay taxes, yet they had no representatives in the English Parliament!

Five months after Thomas Paine had landed in Philadelphia he was listening to a crowd talking excitedly of a battle in Lexington, near Boston. Paine's eyes gleamed bright as he heard of the armed encounter between colonists and British soldiers on Concord Bridge. He felt that he belonged here in America, for the democratic ideas springing up here were his ideas also.

When he tried to write what he thought Aitken refused to print his articles. This Scotsman was afraid of insulting his Tory subscribers, who supported British rule. So Thomas Paine wrote a little book, really only a pamphlet of fifty pages. It was called *Common Sense*. Within a few weeks after it was published it was being read in Philadelphia, in Boston, and in Virginia. It went rapidly from hand to hand all through the thirteen colonies.

This small book expressed the beliefs of the colonists themselves. It declared, in ringing language, what they were thinking. It did not petition the king and Parliament humbly and with apologies. It demanded absolute independence. It was like a bugle call.

"O ye that love mankind! Ye that dare oppose not only the tyranny, but also the tyrant, stand forth!"

When George Washington read *Common Sense* he called it "sound doctrine and unanswerable reasons!"

Tattered copies were treasured past all legibility, and then its message was repeated by word of mouth on lonely farms and on frontiers. This pamphlet put into simple yet eloquent form the basic beliefs of all independence-minded colonists, but it was resented by Tories, who supported the king's laws. *Common Sense* proved to be the most important piece of writing in those early revolutionary times. It brought farm boys and townsmen alike to join the new army being formed by George Washington.

Tom Paine received no money from his book, and he wanted none. He was amazed at the effect it had, as war flared up between British troops and the colonists' militia, who were often only young men armed with squirrel guns.

Paine heard of the Battle of Long Island, when Americans had to retreat secretly to New York City and were carried safely there, overnight, in the small boats of seamen from Marblehead, Massachusetts. As he went about his work he listened to talk of another battle, this one at White Plains. Then he read of the British capture of Fort Washington, on Manhattan. The outlook for General Washington and his army was very dark.

Thomas Paine could no longer stay away from this struggle. He mounted his horse and rode off to Fort Lee, New Jersey, across the Hudson River from Fort Washington. There he joined General Greene's troops and traveled with the weary men of Washington's army down the westward slope of the high Palisades and across the Jersey meadows.

As rearguard soldiers fought against advancing British redcoats, Thomas Paine retreated with them toward Valley

Forge, Pennsylvania. Frost silvered the autumn countryside. Paine was as cold and hungry as his fellows. In his pocket he carried inkpot, goosequill pen, and paper, and as he sat beside a fire each night he wrote with his paper placed on the head of a drum. In this way another pamphlet gradually took form, the first of a series which he called the "Crisis Papers."

"These are the times that try men's souls," he read aloud to the men around him. "The summer soldier and the sunshine patriot will, in this crisis, shrink from the service of their country; but he that stands it *now*, deserves the love and thanks of man and woman."

This pamphlet was printed in Philadelphia after the army had settled in for its first winter at Valley Forge. During those long, agonizing months it was read by soldiers, townsmen, and farmers throughout the colonies. Struggling Americans took courage from the "Crisis Papers." In the struggle for freedom Thomas Paine, more than any other writer, wrote both for the people and to them. He was the spokesman of independence. He was the "Voice of the Revolution."

Copies of Paine's pamphlets were printed and circulated by the thousands. When the war ended and the colonies were free to make a new nation called the United States of America,

Thomas Paine was respected and honored to the far frontiers. New York State gave him a farm in New Rochelle, and Pennsylvania made him a gift of money, for he still wrote without recompense. He chose, however, to live in Bordentown, New Jersey, on the Delaware River.

He was a restless man, easily angered at injustice. He was also blunt and so outspoken that he made as many enemies as friends. He was not the man to lead a quiet life in peace. He accepted an appointment to be secretary of a commission sent out by Congress to establish treaties with the Indians. Then he tried several other positions with the government. These activities did not satisfy him, however, and instead he began to design an iron bridge. In 1787 Paine took his bridge model to England, where he remained for several years.

In England Thomas Paine, who had had only three or four years of regular schooling, became the friend of the great and

powerful in London. And he was as well, if not better, educated than most of them. Along with his democratic beliefs he kept his concern for the poor and unfortunate. When Edmund Burke, orator of the House of Commons, wrote a highly critical book about the French Revolution, then taking place, Paine wrote a book in answer to it. This was the celebrated *Rights of Man,* which he dedicated to George Washington.

Paine stated that men are born free and always continue free and equal in respect to their rights. He said that these rights are liberty, property, security, and resistance to oppression. The nation is the source of all sovereignty, and all authority is derived from it. He wrote of man's responsibility to his fellow men, and of the nation's responsibility to its citizens. Paine also criticized severely Burke's condemnation of the French Revolution.

Britain was so stirred by this book that Tom Paine lost many of his rich and powerful friends in England. The English government was incensed and it labeled Paine ignorant and a traitor. He was indicted for treason. It was at just this time, that Thomas Paine received word, that in recognition of his defense of French Revolutionary ideas, he had been elected a member of the Revolutionary Convention in France. He decided not to go to Paris to accept this honor and responsibility. Not long after his decision was made there was a hurried knock on his door. William Blake, a poet and painter who was a friend of Paine's, rushed in.

"An order for your arrest has been issued. Tom, you must take the next packet for France!"

Tom Paine drew his heavy dark brows down over his eyes in a scowl as he thought.

"Quickly, Tom! They will be here at any moment."

He went aboard the channel boat just in time and was the last passenger up the gangplank as officers ran onto the dock. Thomas Paine never returned to England.

This democrat thought that in France he could make use of his talents. Yet it was not long before he disagreed with the revolutionists there. He advocated exile instead of death for King Louis XVI and Queen Marie Antoinette. When the king and queen were executed on the guillotine Paine was put in prison by Robespierre, powerful leader of the bloody Reign of Terror. Only the quick action of James Monroe, American ambassador to France, saved Paine's life. When political upsets brought the execution of Robespierre himself more moderate control came in. Thomas Paine took his place again in the French convention.

In 1802, when he was old and weary and in bad health, Thomas Paine returned to America. He had more enemies than

friends, for there had been an outcry against his religious beliefs after he published his *Rights of Man*. For a time he lived on his farm in New Rochelle, and then he moved to a lodging house in New York City.

He scarcely knew this America—it had changed so much. People talked of free land for the taking in the South and the West. The United States was striding into a new century, one in which it was to grow to be a great nation. This was to be a century of progress in invention and wealth. The political independence and freedom of thought and speech for which Paine had written so eloquently were taken for granted now. This country no longer needed a Thomas Paine to stir it to resistance. He was an almost forgotten man.

People did not know who he was as he walked slowly along the busy New York City waterfront. A few years later Tom Paine died in a shabby lodging house, and it is not known where his grave is located. He died believing that his writings would be forgotten as he thought that he had been. Not long before his death he wrote to one of his few friends that in all his work his motives and object had been "to rescue man from tyranny and false systems and false principles of government, and enable him to be free."

Through the writings of Thomas Paine the "Voice of the American Revolution" is still heard. It will remain a real part of democracy and of political freedom everywhere.

I Take My Stand

ELIJAH PARISH LOVEJOY

The village of Albion was no more than a cluster of small farmhouses huddled together as if for protection from the Maine wilderness. One lonely farm was closer to the forest than the others. This was the Lovejoy place, settled in 1790 by a trapper whose home was there before the village came. The trapper was the grandfather of Elijah Parish Lovejoy, who was born in 1802.

Elijah grew up knowing as much of beaver and muskrat streams, of the ways of the fox and the mink, as had his grandfather. He was the eldest of the seven children of Daniel and Elizabeth Lovejoy. His father was a Congregational minister as well as a farmer. Elijah spent his days felling trees, grubbing stumps, removing rocks, chopping stovewood for the long, cold winters, plowing and harvesting. He went to a country school only a few months out of the year, when the farm and the forest were covered with snow.

In summer Elijah, his brothers, and other boys always found time to fish and swim in Lovejoy Pond. He was good in sports and was the leader of every adventure. Some grown-ups thought him foolhardy, and said, "That boy will get killed. You

mark my words!" It was Elijah who always dived first into deep water holes and came up with a handful of mud and clams to prove his courage.

One day the boys were arguing beside a lake.

"Nobody can swim across. It's most a mile wide."

Elijah flung off his clothes and dived in. His brothers held their breath with excitement as he swam out with powerful strokes. The boys then ran around the lake and arrived panting just in time to meet Elijah swimming in to shore.

In the farmhouse of an evening his head was buried in a book most of the time. He had such a quick mind and good memory that his mother, who taught him more than his school did, was often amazed. Elijah reluctantly laid aside his books for family prayers, which were long. Although his parents needed his help on the farm they soon realized that this son was meant for

learning. They wanted him to become a minister of the gospel.

"Daniel, Elijah wishes to go to the academy."

"I know. I have been thinking about it for a long time. I don't know how we'll do it, but we will send him there somehow."

From the academy Elijah went on to Waterville College, where he made a record that gained the attention of his teachers. After he graduated he decided that the West was a place that needed a man of religious views and education, and so he accepted the editorship of a newspaper in St. Louis, Missouri. He had expected that, out here on the frontier, such a job would be a challenge to him. Instead, it turned out to be routine, and he thought that what he really wanted was to study for the ministry. His parents rejoiced when they received a letter from Elijah telling them that he was going to Princeton, New Jersey, to attend a theological school. Their son would devote his life to God.

When Lovejoy left Princeton with a theological degree he was offered the choice of several church pastorships, for he was a young Presbyterian minister with a brilliant mind and a fine record. For a short time he served as pastor of a prosperous New York City church, but it did not satisfy him. An easy life was not for him. He wanted to go back to the frontier, for he was a missionary in spirit. He wanted to print and speak the truth, no matter how unpopular it might be. He went back to St. Louis to be editor of a small religious newspaper. This was 1833 and he was thirty-one years old. His parents encouraged him, for they were missionaries in spirit too.

Lovejoy's paper was *The St. Louis Observer*, serving both Presbyterian and Congregationalists of Missouri. Elijah worked during the week in his small office and print shop, where he operated the little press with his own hands. He wrote editorials and religious news and some comments on local events. Then, every weekend, he mounted his horse and rode out to preach on a circuit that took him from crossroads villages to farming communities.

One Saturday Elijah stood on the deck of a steamboat, on his way to a landing upriver on the Mississippi, where he was to preach. As the vessel swung along, fighting the current, he saw the green forests of the Illinois shore. A man leaning on the rail next to him called out, "That's the land of liberty!"

Lovejoy said nothing, but he was coming to agree with this point of view. He had never taken any part in the growing agitation to abolish slavery, and he had no real thought of doing so now. At this time he was writing editorials in the

Observer advising a gradual freeing of slaves by their owners. He thought that as many slaves as possible should be sent back to Africa. Slavery was wrong—and yet he feared that forced emancipation, which the abolitionists were calling for, would bring terrible bloodshed to the country. He believed earnestly in Christianity and just as earnestly in peace.

As he rode or walked from place to place to preach he became aware that slaves were often treated more brutally than in the plantation South. And as he wrote for his paper and worked on the little press Lovejoy became more disturbed and angry at the things he saw and heard about slavery and violence. Other newspapers ignored these acts of violence, but Lovejoy wrote about every one. He frightened his more timid readers, but there were some who approved. When some subscriptions were canceled and protests came in, the owners of the paper came to the editor.

"Look here, Lovejoy, a lot of people don't like the way you are writing on anti-slavery. Can't you just let it ride for a while—just don't write about it so much, or so strongly? Because, if you won't do this there is going to be trouble. Our readers don't want an abolitionist editor."

"I'm not an abolitionist. I am appealing only to the masters of the slaves. I am not urging slaves to rebel."

In 1835 Elijah Lovejoy met Celia Ann French. She lived with her widowed mother in St. Charles which was one of the small towns where he sometimes went to preach. Both were strongly anti-slavery. They invited the minister to their home for dinner, and soon became his friends. Later that year Elijah and Celia were married. Celia had to stay with her mother much of the time, and Elijah went to St. Charles as often as he could manage. As yet he had no money to support a home for his wife in St. Louis. During the long hot summer Celia was ill with cholera. Elijah was seldom in good health himself, but he was determined, and he continued to ride out to preach on Sundays and to write and print his paper during the week.

The Citizens Committee and the Vigilantes of St. Louis warned him to stop printing editorials on slavery, but he paid no attention to them. He was in physical danger himself now, for he had received threats of tarring and feathering and being ridden out of town on a rail. He knew that he might be killed, yet his paper continued to print protests about the treatment of

slaves. With every threat Lovejoy was moving closer to the conviction that slavery must end immediately.

One day a friend walked into the *Observer* office. "Elijah, news is going around that you are having copies of that abolitionist sheet, *The Emancipator,* sent into Missouri. You know this is a slave state!" *The Emancipator* was the official paper published by the American Antislavery Society.

"I have never had *The Emancipator* sent into this state. I try to write the truth in my paper. And I shall continue to do so."

The next issue of *The Observer* carried a statement by the editor:

"I am not aware that any law of my country forbids my sending what document I please to a friend or citizen. I know, indeed that *mob law* has decided otherwise. . . . The truth is,

51

my fellow citizens, if you give ground a single inch there is no stopping place. I deem it, therefore, my duty to take my stand upon the Constitution. Here is firm ground."

When Celia told her husband that they were going to have a child he managed, somehow, to bring her to St. Louis to be with him all the time. They had few comforts in their house, but still it was a home. One night, two years later, Lovejoy was working late in his office when a crowd of rowdies pushed into the little room and threw themselves on him. He was dragged outside to the street, where he saw a bucket of hot tar and a barrel of feathers waiting for him. As he struggled to prevent his attackers from ripping off his clothing, there was a shout beyond the ring of menacing men. Several citizens ran up, guns leveled.

"Let that man go! All right, now. Leave him alone!"

The mob slunk away, and Lovejoy returned to his office. The rescuers were his friends, who respected him although they did not always share his views. But they told him that they might not be able to save him the next time.

The Observer was in trouble. Cancelled subscriptions had been the start of the difficulties, and there was a debt of five hundred dollars. The owners decided to stop printing the paper and asked Lovejoy to resign. He prepared to move to Illinois, but first he went to the man who had made the five-hundred-dollar loan to the paper and signed a note making himself responsible personally for payment. He had no paper to edit now, but he would see what he could do across the Mississippi River.

Just as Lovejoy finished packing his own papers and books he heard the office door slam. The friend who held the note stood there. He was shaking his head, as if he did not really know

why he was doing this for he did not expect to get his money.

"Lovejoy, I've decided to risk my five hundred dollars and keep you on as editor."

For the first time in weeks a smile crept into Elijah's eyes. When his friend had gone he sat down to write the next issue.

In the spring of the following year a savage mob broke into a jail and brutally murdered a Negro prisoner. As Lovejoy wrote about it tears ran down his face onto the paper. He was the only editor in Missouri who so much as mentioned this illegal act of violence. Again he was threatened, and now he was in constant fear for the safety of his wife and son. At last Elijah Lovejoy decided he must dismantle his small press and move it across to Illinois which was not a slave state. That day, as he was taking the press apart to be shipped a crowd pushed into the shop, shouting, "We'll help you get this thing out. Let's go, boys!"

As Lovejoy watched helplessly his press was carried to the river and thrown into muddy water. Next day Elijah got a secret loan from a friend and bought another press, ordering it to be sent to Alton, Illinois.

He took his wife and child across the river and settled them in a small house just outside the town. Lovejoy waited impatiently for his press to arrive. He believed that here, in a state that did not permit slavery, he could publish and distribute his religious paper safely.

Lovejoy arranged to have his press arrive in Alton on Sunday, when it would not attract attention, but instead it came the next day. By Monday morning Alton was seething with talk. There was an active anti-slavery group in the town, but it numbered only a few men and women. Most of the townsmen believed in slavery, although they lived in an anti-slavery state.

As the steamboat tied up, Lovejoy, who was ill, came to the dock, which was jammed with belligerent men. As the crate was lifted to shore a yell went up,

"There it is! Get it!"

The editor and his friends were nearly pushed into the river as rioters leaped forward, grabbed the crate and threw it into the water. Lovejoy, pale as death, went home. That evening a few grim men gathered at his house and told him that they were collecting money to buy him another press.

When the next printing press arrived there was no trouble. The town seemed to be waiting in a deadly quiet—like

the strange stillness before a hurricane strikes. The new press was set up in Lovejoy's office, and he went to work. For several months Elijah and Celia enjoyed a peace they had not known before. Then the editor distributed a petition calling for action in Congress against slavery and appealed for a state antislavery society. Lovejoy was immediately threatened on the street and in his office.

One hot night in August he went to the drugstore to get a bottle of medicine for Celia and the baby who were both ill. He was walking slowly home to his cottage when an icy feeling of fear crept over him. Those men approaching—who were they? He was in the middle of the road and they were coming toward him with menace in the very way they strode along. As always Lovejoy controlled his fear and continued advancing calmly. As he reached them they moved aside. Lovejoy drew a deep breath of relief and continued toward his house. Then he heard footsteps behind him and looked over his shoulder. They were still there, but had turned around and were following him. As he came to the edge of the town the men closed in around him. Lovejoy held out the bottle of medicine.

"I will offer no resistance. But I will be grateful to you if you will take this medicine to my sick wife and child."

One man slowly took the bottle and started toward the cottage with it. Lovejoy could see a single lamp burning in his home. The other men were silent, and Lovejoy felt that confusion and uncertainty had replaced the feeling of menace. Suddenly one man swung on his heel and left. The others followed. Lovejoy went home. It was that same night that another mob broke into his shop and destroyed his new press.

A group of citizens once more sent for a press, and when it arrived in November they were ready to receive it and give it protection.

Lovejoy and his friend, Winthrop Gilman, asked Mayor Krum to form a military company to defend civil rights.

"I agree that Alton needs a militia company to prevent a riot," said the mayor. "I cannot form one—but you can. It is lawful for private citizens to call up a militia as Alton does not have one."

Gilman formed a small military company to protect the press. Forty-two citizens volunteered. Some believed in slavery, but they also believed more strongly in the Constitutional right of freedom of the press. Gilman was part owner of a warehouse near the river, and they planned to keep the press under guard there until it was safe to use it. The warehouse seemed easy to defend. It was built of stone, with windows only in the two gables, one facing the river and the other looking on Water Street.

As the crate was brought into the warehouse the guards let out a shout that echoed against the rafters. These men were equipped with rifles and shotguns and were ready to stand off any mob that might come. When no rioters appeared twenty guards went home, leaving only a few men on watch through the night.

At sunset Elijah Lovejoy walked slowly home, worrying about Celia and the baby. The town looked deserted. There were no women and children on the streets. An occasional man appeared frozen in his position as the editor passed. In spite of himself Elijah began to hurry. Friends had brought word to him at the warehouse that the gang of rowdies might attack his house. Although he knew the house was guarded, fear gripped him fiercely. Yet when he came into the cottage he found Celia putting their son to bed. She was very white, but she smiled as she put his supper on the table.

On the following evening, November 7, 1837, with the town still quiet, Lovejoy joined eighteen men guarding the press in the warehouse. He was hoping it would not be long until it would be safe to take it to his shop and set it up for work. Until ten o'clock that night the men talked calmly in the light of several lamps upstairs. Abruptly a loud pounding shook the front doors.

"What do you want out there?" Each man just inside the door was holding his gun cocked.

"Give up that press or we'll break down the doors!"

Gilman shouted, "No. And don't try to take it. We've

got guns here! And we will use them if you force us to do it."

A hail of rocks hit the stone walls of the warehouse. Gilman ran upstairs and yelled from a window, telling the men to go away. He saw that there were more than two hundred out in the street, and he caught sight of many firearms. Gilman beat a hasty retreat downstairs. Before he reached the bottom of the stairs stones crashed into the windows. The defenders went up and crouched beside the broken windows, guns leveled. Lamps were darkened. A shot splintered a windowsill. Answering fire scattered the attackers. A man outside yelled in pain and then crumpled and was carried away. There was a brief silence. Then the mob formed again, and surrounded the building. Lovejoy

stared out, wondering why? There were no windows on the sides.

Mayor Krum, a judge, and several peace officers were trying outside to persuade the mob to disperse. When they failed, the mayor was let inside the warehouse.

"They mean business," he said grimly. "If we don't let them have the press there will be a pitched battle."

One guard answered for all of them. He said that if the mob got the printing press it would have to get them first.

Suddenly a strange silence fell outside. Lovejoy raised his head, sniffing smoke. A church bell clanged and rang in the town. An elderly woman, an invalid, had dragged herself to the Presbyterian church and was ringing the bell in a frantic call for help for the besieged in the warehouse. The sound only infuriated the wild mob, and yelling broke loose once more.

"Fire! The roof's on fire!"

Gray wisps were seeping through roof cracks into the building as fire burst out above. Someone had climbed a ladder and set a torch to the old wooden shingles. The defenders opened the doors, and some of them charged into the rioters, scattering them. Lovejoy, with two others, ran to the open doors and leveled their pistols at the man on the ladder. Lovejoy was clearly outlined by moonlight. Shots, fired from behind a pile of lumber, were not even heard in the uproar. Elijah Lovejoy, hit by five bullets, staggered inside the warehouse and collapsed on the stairway to the second floor. His companions rushed to him. Then one stepped to the open doorway. There was no longer any reason to hold out.

"We surrender! Lovejoy is dead."

The defenders left the building and were peppered with buckshot as they ran for cover. A gang of the attackers destroyed the press with sledge hammers and cast the pieces into the Mississippi River. Others put out the roof fire, and defenders and attackers went home. A cold moon shone on a town without a newspaper.

In the months that followed the name of Elijah Lovejoy came to be respected by many who did not share his beliefs as well as by those who did. He had refused to surrender to a mob his Constitutional right to write as he believed and to print a newspaper according to his own principles.

As Good as a Boy

ELIZABETH CADY STANTON

Sunlight was bright on the millpond water. Elizabeth and her younger sister Margaret stood on the shore looking at a raft swinging gently in the current by a rope tied to an overhanging tree.

The little girls made a bright picture against the green foliage for they were dressed alike in red frocks, with white neck ruffles, black aprons and shoes, and red stockings. Elizabeth gave her skirt an irritated jerk. She hated red. It was her mother's favorite color, and Elizabeth and her sisters had to wear it every day until they were twelve years old and became young ladies. Even on Sunday their dresses were scarlet but with a black sprigged pattern, and they wore red cloaks and hoods. Nobody in Johnstown, in upper New York state, could fail to recognize one of the daughters of Judge Cady.

And there was nobody in town, thought Elizabeth, who had failed to say of the Cady children, "Too bad! Four girls and only one boy."

Every day after school Elizabeth and Margaret ran to the millpond to watch their older brother and his friends float the raft around calm water above the falls. But today the boys had not come. Elizabeth looked over her shoulder. Only Peter, the Negro servant boy, was there with them as always, and he had his face lifted to look at a bird singing on a branch of a wild cherry tree.

Elizabeth whispered to her sister, "Come on. This is our chance."

The two little girls jumped on the raft. As Elizabeth untied the rope Margaret hugged herself in glee. Elizabeth could do anything, Margaret thought, that a boy could do. She had been told that often enough by her sister when she and Elizabeth climbed secretly out on the roof outside their room and sat there whispering in the moonlight.

"Miss Lizabeth! Don't you do that! You'll get killed!"

Peter's anguished voice came to the adventurers as the raft swung out of calm water into the millpond current. Elizabeth grasped the heavy steering pole and pulled until her arms hurt. Margaret crawled over and tried to help, but they could not manage it. Margaret began to cry. Her sister gritted her teeth and yanked on the pole with her plump arms until her face grew as scarlet as her dress.

Peter's voice no longer came to them, but now they heard their brother shouting as he ran along the shore, "Watch out! You're headed for the falls."

The raft floated around helplessly, gave a lurch, and plunged over the dam. The two girls clung to the heavy pole, and shut their eyes. When they opened them they were still on the raft, and it was right side up in the stream below the dam. Peter, his face gray, was wading out with their brother to bring them safely to land.

64

In the Cady household in 1815, when Elizabeth was
ten, discipline was stern. Yet Elizabeth's merry blue eyes were
seldom darkened by the discipline for, although she feared her
parents' wrath when she misbehaved, she loved and respected
them both. She was next to the youngest in the family, and also the
liveliest and most adventurous. While the older two girls were
away at the seminary for young ladies or were entertaining their
many beaux, the younger girls roamed the countryside. They
played in the dusty barn or rode their horses. On rainy days they
crept up to the forbidden attic to dress in their mother's old
clothes and to eat apples and nuts from the barrels stored there, or
nibble maple sugar cakes from the shelves. In winter they were
wrapped in buffalo robes for sleigh rides or they skimmed down
hills on sleds, and skated on the frozen pond.

65

Although she led a happy life, Elizabeth was the only one of the four girls who wished that she had been a boy. When her hand was slapped sharply by her nurse because she fingered her stiff, scratchy neck ruffles, she wailed, "Why should I have to wear this thing?" Her older sisters dressed as they pleased, for they were young ladies, but no amount of protest could make any change in the red, black, and white costumes of Elizabeth and Margaret.

Their constant guide and helper was Peter, who was a few years older than they. Everywhere the girls went Peter was there to look after them. He was trustworthy, kind, and gentle, and always full of fun. Elizabeth felt that Peter was "the only thing, visible or invisible, of whom we had no fear." Sometimes in the evening Elizabeth, Margaret, and Peter sat on the hearth in the big kitchen, listening to the Negro servants, Abraham and Jacob, as they played guitars and sang.

When they went to church, Peter, who followed behind them, turned aside and climbed to the balcony to sit while the family walked to the Cady pew. Elizabeth resented this. Why couldn't Peter sit with the family? And so, one Sunday, she marched solemnly to the balcony behind Peter and sat down beside him. It made no difference that Peter hastily took her back down to her amazed family. She had told the townspeople, and especially her parents, how she felt about an injustice.

When her father and mother were most angry at her disobedience they talked to her sternly of the wrath of God. Sometimes she dreamed of the devil and the fires of hell and awakened Margaret with her cries. It was no wonder that she hated a frock the color of flames. Elizabeth's fear of God was so great that she

66

disliked the clanging of church bells. Johnstown was filled with the sound on Sunday, and Elizabeth felt that she could not escape them, for she was a guilty sinner.

When Elizabeth was eleven years old tragedy struck the home of Judge Cady. The one son of the family became very ill, and the best medical care in Johnstown could not save him. Although Judge Cady was a member of Congress as well as a wealthy and distinguished lawyer, nothing in his life seemed to mean much to him after that.

On the day after the funeral Elizabeth went into her father's library and saw him sitting with his head in his hands. She climbed into his lap and heard him sigh as his hand smoothed her hair, "Oh, how I wish you were a boy!"

His daughter threw her arms around his neck, crying, "I will be just like a boy, Father!"

Elizabeth seemed to grow up more quickly after that day. She was quieter, with a determined look in her round, rosy face. How could she be like a boy? There were two things that her brother had done especially well—riding and learning Greek. Elizabeth got Peter to give her riding lessons every day, and she went to the minister and asked him to teach her Greek. It was the custom to keep girls at home after they finished grammar school, or to send them for a short time to a "finishing school" to learn dancing, music, painting, embroidery, and manners. Elizabeth was not interested in these accomplishments.

When she could ride as well as her brother had and read Greek as well as any boy in town, she asked her father to test her in both. She expected him to say proudly, "You are as good as a boy." But he smiled sadly and said quietly, "You are a good horse-woman and a bright girl, Elizabeth," and turned away.

After that Elizabeth began to appear often at her father's law office. She became something of a nuisance to the law students there, for she read so many of the difficult books and asked so many questions.

One day, as she sat in a corner reading she heard Flora Campbell telling the judge that she was without money, although she had brought considerable wealth to her husband when they married. Elizabeth had always known Mrs. Campbell as a wealthy woman, and she was amazed to hear her say, "He will not give me enough to live on, Judge Cady, or proper clothing, although he spends my money for fine horses and rich living himself."

Elizabeth could scarcely believe her ears when she heard her father reply that a married woman had no legal rights to property of her own, not even her jewelry. As Judge Cady escorted Mrs. Campbell out he saw his daughter furiously tearing from one of her father's books the pages on which these unfair laws were printed.

"Elizabeth," he shouted, "Stop that! Come into my office."

Judge Cady told her she would do no good to anyone by tearing up his valuable law books. The only way to help women achieve equality in law was to get the state legislature to change the laws. He explained that the United States Constitution itself gave the right to vote only to white men—not to idiots, lunatics, criminals, Negroes, or women. As Elizabeth walked home along the tree-shaded streets of Johnstown she made three resolutions. She would do anything that she could to free Negro slaves. She

would help women to become legally equal to men. And she would grow up to be just as good as a man.

When Elizabeth was fifteen she went to Troy, New York, to attend Miss Emma Willard's Seminary, although she wanted to go with the boys to Union College. She traveled on the first railroad that had been built in the United States. On her arrival she found that, although she knew far more than the other students—and even more than some teachers in certain subjects— she was far behind the other girls in French, dancing, and music. She spent two years at the Seminary, made many friends, and learned the ladylike arts and accomplishments, but she felt that her real knowledge was not so great. Yet Miss Willard was a pioneer in women's education, and her school was one of the best in the country.

For ten years Elizabeth lived at home, adapting herself to womanly tasks and social life. Her older sisters were married, and her mother was not well. Elizabeth was naturally energetic and efficient, and she was soon in charge of the household. She went with young men to dances and picnics and joined in the fun of music and parlor games. She was often the leader of pranks played on the beaux who flocked to the Cady house to see the two girls. Yet discussions of problems of the state and the nation between her father and his older friends were of more interest to her.

Johnstown was an intellectual center. Visitors brought news of the growing antislavery movement and of their part in it. One of these visitors was young Henry B. Stanton, who seemed to prefer the conversation of Miss Elizabeth to that of her father. He came often, and the two took long walks and buggy rides together. No one was surprised when Mr. Stanton asked Judge Cady for his daughter's hand in marriage. Nor was anyone who knew Elizabeth astonished when, in the wedding ceremony, the word "obey" was not mentioned.

Soon after their marriage in 1840 the Stantons sailed for London, England, to attend an antislavery convention. Women were not permitted at the meetings, except to sit in a curtained loft to listen. Elizabeth sitting there, found herself beside Mrs. Lucretia Mott, a Quakeress.

"While men talk of freedom for Negro slaves, we women are treated as if we were the harem wives of Turks. Freedom for women is just as important."

"Yes indeed, Mrs. Stanton. I quite agree with you."

The two ladies talked of action to correct this injustice and discussed plans. Yet Elizabeth had to postpone doing anything, for she returned to America to establish a home for her husband and to have a child.

70

Elizabeth and her husband went to live in Chelsea, Massachusetts. For some time Elizabeth was so busy with motherhood that she thought of little else. There were problems here too. The nurse wrapped the baby in such tight swaddling blankets that he could not move his legs. Elizabeth had some new ideas on baby care. When Elizabeth unwrapped the baby and let him kick, the nurse frowned, predicted disaster, and wrapped him up again.

In 1847 the Stantons moved to Seneca Falls, New York. Now there were more children, and managing the large house and grounds, the servants, and the family took all Elizabeth's time.

Then one day, when she went to see a friend, she found another visitor who greeted her with a smile. It was Lucretia Mott. Other women came in that afternoon, and before going home Elizabeth Stanton had joined them in organizing a convention in Seneca Falls. Next day the local newspaper printed an announcement of the convention "to discuss the social, civil, and religious condition of women."

This convention was held in July, 1848. Elizabeth Stanton was fortunate, for she was one of the few women whose husbands gave approval to this "wild and unwomanly act." Standing firmly on the platform Mrs. Stanton read her "Declaration of Sentiments." This was phrased like the Declaration of Independence, but she had added "and women" to the statement that all men are created equal.

It was the first open and formal plea for woman suffrage, or the right to vote, ever voiced in the United States. Even the older women present thought that it went too far, yet, since

Mrs. Stanton talked so well and so persuasively it was adopted. Elizabeth was still saying to the world, "Girls are as good as boys. Women are as intelligent as men."

This resolution raised a storm in pulpit and press all across the nation. Although most of the women at the meeting were wives and mothers, preachers condemned, politicians roared, and newspapers screamed that such sentiments came only from "sour old maids and childless females." Many of the women who had signed the document withdrew their names.

Elizabeth Cady Stanton took it all as a challenge. She had not expected approval. She was a fighter, and she knew that most women, whether they said so or not, secretly sympathized. There were a few friendly newspapers, and to these she sent articles, citing history, law, and science to bolster her views. People laughed and shouted, "Cackling roosters and crowing hens will always come to some bad end!"

Elizabeth was coming to be called Cady Stanton most of the time as she became better known. She met another Quakeress, Susan B. Anthony, a schoolteacher who wanted to work for temperance, women's rights, and the abolition of slavery. She was a good executive, calm and quiet in her actions, and she and Elizabeth worked well together. Cady Stanton wrote fiery articles, while Susan Anthony was the planner and handled the organizational work. Both of them set out on crusades all over the country. They traveled from town to city to village, speaking, sometimes together and sometimes separately.

The Civil War brought their activities for women's rights temporarily to an end. In 1867, after the war was over, they went back to women's suffrage work. That year Kansas was putting to the vote a new constitution which would, if passed, allow Negro men, and also "the less muscular sex," both Negro and white, to vote. Cady and Susan made speeches throughout Kansas.

They did not really expect the new constitution to win, but they were pleased when one third of the voters put it on record that they wanted votes for women.

Mrs. Stanton and Miss Anthony started a newspaper. They were joined by another famous suffragette, Lucy Stone, who believed that a woman should keep her own name after marriage. Cady did not think that so important. It made no difference to her what name she bore just so long as she could speak and write and work for the vote. When she couldn't get enough household help she rocked a cradle with one hand as she wrote with the other. Or she sat up late in the night to write after her children were in bed. Susan often wondered how Cady could write so clearly and strongly with so many interruptions. Her busy friend only laughed.

"I enjoy making a pudding or dressing a child just as much as I like to lecture or write an article. I am thankful for the opportunity to do both."

For three years the thoughtful and lively pen of Cady Stanton helped keep the publication going. When funds gave out, however, the paper had to close. Yet she had the satisfaction of knowing that her work had influenced many people.

During the next twelve years Cady Stanton worked with the Woman's Suffrage Association and also went on speaking tours into distant parts of the country. She traveled in carriages, and sometimes in wagons, when there was no railroad available.

Country hotels at that time were dirty, cold, or stifling hot, and the food was bad. There was one night when the hotel was so uncomfortable that Mrs. Stanton decided to sleep in her traveling carriage. She was soon awakened by grunting noises

beneath her. Then the floor of the carriage began to bump up and down alarmingly. Taking a lantern she looked beneath and saw several razorback hogs rolling about. Tired as she was, she was so angry that she grasped the whip and lashed at them. They fled, squealing. She had no sooner dozed again than the noise and bumping started once more.

After that Mrs. Stanton braved the hotel's discomforts with more patience. She endured all this, as well as the jeers and insults of hostile crowds, for she knew that more and more women were coming silently to listen to her. Their presence in the crowd meant more than the mocking laughter of the rowdy men who were there also.

As the years passed Elizabeth Cady Stanton and Susan B. Anthony came to be respected. Nevertheless it was an uphill fight. Everywhere they went for years they were followed by a trail of laughter, abuse, and scorn. Mrs. Stanton was elected president of the Woman's Suffrage Association, a position she held until 1893 when she was seventy-eight years of age. She then gave up her office to devote all her time to writing. With Susan B. Anthony and another fellow worker she published the *History of Woman Suffrage*. Her autobiography was published in 1898. Through these years she ran her home carefully, and the seven Stanton children grew up to be a credit to their parents.

Mrs. Stanton also lectured on new and improved methods of housework, better ways of preparing food, and child care. When she was eighty years old Elizabeth Cady Stanton was given a birthday party at the Metropolitan Opera House in New York. At the end of her speech, as she looked at the faces turned to her, and then up to the balconies and boxes filled with people who had come to do her honor, she suddenly thought of her father. He had never said, "Elizabeth, you are as good as a boy." Yet he had always given his approval of her efforts to change the harsh laws making women the property of men and refusing them the right to vote as citizens. She realized, standing there on the stage, what a fortunate woman she had been, for she had also had a husband who was loyal and who had believed in her crusade.

By 1896, Elizabeth Cady Stanton had the joy of knowing that several states had given women the vote. Before she died in 1902 she knew, too, that a few women had become doctors and lawyers, as well as teachers, professional artists, writers, and business women. The door had been opened to opportunity for them. An amendment to the Constitution of the United States, allowing women to vote, was passed June 5th, 1919.

Who could doubt that the spirit of Elizabeth Cady was present on that day, and that all three resolutions made by the little girl in the scarlet dress had been fulfilled.

The Shoes of Happiness

EDWIN MARKHAM

It was the quiet time at the end of the day, just before Mrs. Markham closed the store. She was used to looking after her husband's store as well as their home, for Markham spent most of his time working on his farm. Housewives of the village of Oregon City had gone home to build fires in their wood-burning stoves for supper. The baby on the floor solemnly chewed on a cracker.

"Tell us about the stampede, Ma," begged Edwin, as he sat on an apple barrel behind the counter.

"You know it by heart already, son. How about hearing of the Indian attack on the wagon train? Or how cholera struck us down on the Platte River? You want that stampede too often."

Edwin just waited. He was only four years old, but he knew that his mother liked to tell stories of her trip west in 1850 with her husband, the wagon master. She sat down in a rocker to enjoy her few moments of rest, and the baby reached up to be lifted into her lap. As she spoke the chair made a squeaking accompaniment to her voice.

"That morning I was alone at the spring. It was early dawn, and the hunters already out chasing a herd of buffalo. As far as the eye could see there was nothing on the grassy plains but the wagon circle in the distance. I filled my bucket and turned to tote it back when a noise like thunder broke on me. I was scared stiff and couldn't move. Before I knew it there were the beasts, stampeding right at me! I threw myself flat on my face. Those buffaloes ran straight over me, but the Lord held me in his hand. When your father found me all I had was three broken ribs—and after I took some strips of a petticoat and tied myself up so tight I could hardly breathe, I went back to my work. We were on our way from Michigan to Oregon, and in those days a woman on the trail didn't take any ease just for broken ribs."

Edwin Markham's early memories were nearly all of his mother. He was born in Oregon in 1852. His cradle was a hollowed-out log, made by his father. The Markham ancestors were true pioneers, coming to America before the Revolution and moving westward as the wilderness began to open up. Edwin's mother was a pioneer wife, and one who brought wide knowledge as well as great energy to the life of the small community in which she lived. She had brought along a bag of apple seeds and with them had planted one of the first orchards in the northwest.

When she was not telling the two boys about the long trail westward she was reading poems to them from the few books in the house. Mrs. Markham had a talent for writing. She sent poems to the local newspapers. There wasn't a wedding, funeral, birth, or any other event, from the Fourth of July to Christmas, that she did not commemorate with a poem. She wrote also about the birds and the plants of the region. She often sat by a coal-oil lamp in the evening, writing in neat script on cheap paper.

Edwin was about five when his father grew restless at

exciting news of a new gold strike in California. Mr. Markham put his family into the wagon, and they rolled down into the Suisun Valley not far from Sacramento. There they bought a small ranch, which Mrs. Markham ran while her husband was away prospecting. As he grew older Edwin was her chief helper. They had a few sheep and, later on, a herd of cattle.

Sometimes, when it was hot and dry in the valley, Edwin drove the small flock of sheep into the hills to find pasture. On such a day, as he came from the little ranch house at dawn, he never failed to stand a few moments facing the east to watch the first light outlining the peaks of the Sierra Nevada mountains in the distance. As his bare feet followed his flock up into low hills he stopped now and then to pick handfuls of wild berries and stuff them into his mouth. Edwin soon knew every cold river and each stand of trees in these hills as well as he knew the grassy valley and the blue lake which the hills surrounded. As grass turned green in the valley he pastured his sheep there. He worked in his mother's vegetable garden and plowed and harvested in their few fields.

He went to school briefly each winter, never for long at a time, but his mother had taught him to read. When he was eight years old he read his first book all the way through. It was Peter Parley's *History of the World* for children. Then he read *The Story of the Pyramids* and the Almanac. These, and the Bible, were the only books in his home. Each evening he read the Bible, a few verses at a time, just before going to bed.

The year Edwin was thirteen he attended a country school. This tall gangling boy wanted to learn, and yet he felt uncomfortable and too big for a bench in the little Redwood School. He folded his big hands on the small desk and listened intently to the teacher. Harry G. Hill was also tall and rugged, and he looked as if he too had spent his life outdoors herding sheep and cattle. Nevertheless he held the book of poetry respectfully, and he read poems aloud in a deep, musical voice. After school Edwin went up shyly to ask about the poems, and Mr. Hill loaned him his own books to read at home.

Edwin and his mother lived alone on the ranch now, for both his father, the prospector who had never found a fortune, and his younger brother had died. Though still in his teens Edwin was a farmer, a herder of sheep, and a cowhand. He was a *vaquero,* as the Mexican cowboys were called.

Yet Edwin's mind was filled with poetry. When he left Redwood he went to the Black School for a time. It was from the teacher in that log schoolhouse that he learned what a college was.

Although he saw no way at all of his getting a chance to go to college, he began to dream of it. If he did find a college that would take him, and if by some remote possibility he could pay for it, how could his mother manage on the ranch? At last he got up the courage to tell her.

"I want to go to college, Ma. I can't think about anything else."

His mother carefully set the iron kettle on the stove. Then she said slowly, "You ought to go to college, Edwin. No one knows it better than I do. But how could I run the ranch alone? Maybe later on I could hire a cowhand. College costs money. Where would we get it?"

Edwin bent over his plate. Neither said anything more about going to college. Edwin brooded over it, though. His teacher spoke of the Normal School in San José. This was a teachers' college near San Francisco. One day Edwin could no longer resist his urge to go. He believed his mother could afford to hire a cowhand, and would if he were not there to do everything. That night Edwin slipped out to the barn secretly, saddled his horse, and rode away.

He said to himself, "I'll ride in the direction I know

least about, toward the blue coast range." The trail led west.

His first days were carefree and happy. He knew how to live on the country, shooting rabbits and squirrels for his frying pan, building a quick fire, sleeping on the ground under the towering trees. He refused to be discouraged by the fact that he did not have a cent to his name. It would take him a while to get to college, but he would find ranch jobs and save his wages.

One night as he sat by his fire, leaning close to the flame to read one of the books from his saddlebags, he heard the pounding of horses' hooves. Three men pulled up. A bearded fellow jumped down and drew his pistol.

"It's a holdup!"

"Well—I've got nothing but books."

The bandits shoved their weapons back in their holsters when they found Edwin was unarmed. Then they hunkered down by the fire. The bearded highwayman was curious. He said that he admired somebody who could read and asked Edwin to show him how well he did it. Edwin read and was surprised to find that the man didn't want him to stop.

Next morning when Edwin woke up he found his horse saddled along with the others. The leader of the outlaws had his gun drawn again.

"You're going with us, boy. You're going to educate me."

Edwin became the prisoner of the gang. He lived in their camp for several weeks and read aloud, over and over, every book he had with him. At first this was exciting, but he soon grew tired of the life of a captive. He told the chief that he wanted to go to college and tried to persuade him to let his prisoner

go. After several weeks of persuasion the outlaw suddenly nodded, told him to leave when he liked, and tried to give him money. Edwin refused the stolen gold. As he rode off his friends fired their pistols in the air as a farewell salute.

After traveling for several weeks Markham found a ranch and got a temporary job as a cowhand. Then he moved on to another, and another. Luck was not with him, however, for he never made much more than his board and bunk. College seemed a long way off.

Then one day as he rode in from the range, he saw a familiar rusty black carriage drawn by a horse that was an old friend. He wasn't surprised to find his mother in the kitchen swapping recipes with the wife of the ranch owner.

She said dryly, "Well, Edwin, it took me six months to track you down after you ran off. If you'll come home I'll save every last nickel to send you to college."

A week or so after his return with his mother Edwin was digging soap root for his mother's clothes-boiling kettle. He was in a patch of brush out beyond a field where he had often dug before he left home. He turned over a big loose stone, and his eyes popped with surprise. In the hole there was a canvas bag. It looked like a money poke! He shook it; it jingled! He slowly loosened the string and turned it over. Out rolled shining gold pieces. There was more than nine hundred dollars in that bag!

That night he and his mother stared at the gold as it lay in a heap on the kitchen table. "Must be it was hidden by a miner who never came back for it," said Mrs. Markham. Edwin, remembering his outlaw friend, said nothing, but he wondered. Had the bearded robber placed the money there for him? He never found out, but that money made it possible for him to go to college. He decided to apply at the teachers' college in San José.

The college was small and its students serious and hard-working. They lived in rented rooms in San José, and many of them did part-time work in town. Edwin added to his supply of money by plowing fields on nearby farms. His pay from a season's farm work was twenty dollars. He promptly spent it all on books and felt like a millionaire. He owned so few books, and he wanted so many! The first books he bought were Victor Hugo's *Les Miserables* and *The Man Who Laughs*. As he read them over and over again in his tiny room his sympathy went out to the poor of the world and to those who worked so hard for so little. He read the Bible, too, and began to understand better what Jesus meant to the unfortunate.

After a while his mother came to live with him. The money found under the stone did not last through the two years of college. With outside jobs, however, Edwin completed his schooling and looked after his mother also. He graduated at the top of his class, and Mrs. Markham proudly watched him give the valedictory address.

What now? It was 1872, and Edwin Markham was a tall, strong young fellow. He got a teaching position in San Luis Obispo and worked on the side as a blacksmith's helper. There were only nine pupils and he had no schoolhouse. Parents of the students paid him a small salary. How could he teach children without a schoolroom? As Edwin pondered this problem his eyes fell on a great oak tree, and an idea came to him. This ancient tree had enormous, spreading branches with foliage so thick that the rain could not penetrate it. Under this wide umbrella of green leaves the new teacher placed benches and tables which he himself had made of rough lumber. Then he put up a fence of saplings in a circle around the tree. Here he taught his nine pupils. And, as always, he spent every spare cent he could get on books of poetry by Whittier, Byron, Bryant, and Tennyson.

After a while Markham decided to return to college. His mother had moved to El Dorado County and was living alone. He took a graduate degree from Christian College in Santa Rosa. A few years later Markham was appointed head of the Teachers' Training College in Oakland, across the bay from San Francisco. During these years Edwin Markham had been writing poetry as well as reading it, and some of his poems had been published in local newspapers. About this time two of his books were published, *The Shoes of Happiness* and *California the Wonderful*. This beautiful land in which he lived forty years was a theme that always attracted him.

In these early years of teaching Markham married and had a son, but the marriage was unhappy, and a divorce followed. A few years later he met Anna Catherine Murphy, an editor and a poet, who had seen his work in a magazine. His reputation was growing with publication in national magazines. With the help of his new friend, Markham compiled a ten-volume collection called *The Book of Poetry*.

When he asked Catherine to marry him she said, "I've been told never to marry a teacher or a man with a beard, and you are both." Nevertheless, this marriage turned out to be a happy one.

In 1886 Edwin Markham opened a copy of Scribner's Magazine and was fascinated by a picture. It was a reproduction of a painting by a French artist Jean François Millet, called "The Man with a Hoe." It pictured a field and the figure of a worker, bent wearily and hopelessly over his hoe. To the poet, who himself had worked hard with his hands, this peasant seemed never to have had a chance to develop his mind and spirit. Through poverty and unceasing labor he had become more like a patient ox than a human being.

Markham pulled some sheets of paper toward him and began to write a poem. It wasn't easy. The poem was not finished that day, nor for many years. Yet it stayed in his thoughts, and in 1899 he finished it. Like Millet's picture it was called "The Man with the Hoe." The publication of this poem made Edwin Markham famous. It was reprinted in nearly every newspaper of any size in the country; it started arguments in papers and magazines, and stimulated countless sermons and speeches. This was not a pretty poem. Some people disliked it violently, and said so. In

simple but moving words it showed the world how terrible a thing it is to be a slave to constant labor, with no chance to enjoy the beauty of the earth, the stars, or the good things made by man.

Edwin Markham and his wife moved to New York City, and then to a house on Staten Island across the bay. The poet was known throughout the land and was always recognized as he walked the streets of New York. He was a striking figure, with a wide sombrero, such as he had worn as a young *vaquero* in California, crowning his shock of gray hair. Few wives could have adapted to the life that Catherine's husband led, for he often slept by day and walked the streets at night. Sometimes he remained at home and wrote all night, and Catherine, whom he called "the Madonna," had to get used to cooking his meals at odd hours.

The hard life of those who had no education and no opportunities was never out of Markham's thoughts for long. At a time when most people ignored such things, he visited the "sweat shops" of the city, where women and children worked at machines in dark rooms. He took trips to New England and down into the

Southern states to observe pathetic young children who worked in mills instead of going to school. Throughout the country there were thousands who never felt sunlight warm their thin shoulders. In 1903 more than two million children were working in factories, mills, mines, and workshops from four-thirty in the morning until long after dark.

After these journeys, in 1906, Edwin Markham published a brilliant series of articles about working children in *Cosmopolitan Magazine*. He called the series, "The Hoe-Man in the Making."

One of the articles began with the story of an old Indian chief who came to see the grand sights of civilization in New York City. After a tour of Manhattan the chief, considered a savage by white men, was asked, "What is the most surprising thing you have seen?" He answered slowly, "Little children

working." Said Markham, "For the Indian father does not ask his children to work, but leaves them free till the age of maturity, when they are ushered with solemn rites into the obligations of their elders."

Markham wrote of mills in which children under twelve did night work, "The average child lives only four years after it enters the mills. Pneumonia stalks in the damp, lint-filled rooms, and leads hundreds of little ones out to rest. Hundreds more are maimed by the machinery, two or three for each of their elders."

These strong articles caused many people to join the Child Labor Federation and demand reforms. Most of the states passed some protective laws for children. National laws forbidding child labor were not passed until a number of years later. Yet Markham's articles helped bring an end to the enslavement of children in mills, mines, and city sweatshops.

In 1904 Markham had joined other writers to found the first poetry society in the United States. At the dedication of the Lincoln Memorial in Washington, D. C., Edwin Markham was asked to read a poem that he had written about Abraham Lincoln. This poem was later inscribed on the memorial to Lincoln built around the log cabin in Kentucky where the president was born.

Famous people of the world went to Staten Island to the Markham home. They were amused and interested to see that the house was stacked with books from top to bottom. Markham bought so many books from secondhand stores that he even had dusty volumes piled on the stairway. He had read them all and knew them from cover to cover. His thirst for reading was never satisfied.

When asked, "Why so many books, Mr. Markham?" he replied with a smile, "Reading is living. Each book helps me to live some more."

Striding along the streets he carried books in his big pockets, in his hands, or in his briefcase. He was never without them.

On his eightieth birthday a celebration was held in Carnegie Hall for Edwin Markham, the "grand old man of poetry." His friends overflowed the great auditorium as he read his poems. Outside Carnegie Hall, outside New York City as well as in it—all across America, to the mountains and valleys of California—thousands of lives had unknowingly been changed by Edwin Markham. These were children, now free to feel the sun on their faces, free to go to school and to read books, free to wear "the shoes of happiness."

The Whole World in His Hands

MARIAN ANDERSON

The little girl skipped a bit, now and then, to the rhythm of her humming as she went to the grocery store. She was only eight years old, and her head was filled with the sound of music. She was a proud member of the junior choir of her church, and she sang often at home too with her father, whose favorite tune was "Asleep in the Deep." Her mother's voice singing old American songs, hymns, and spirituals seemed a part of all household chores. After her father managed to buy a piano there was more music. Music was good. Music was happy. Music stayed in the head and in the heart and lightened the hard duties of life.

Marian scarcely heard the clatter of horses' hooves on cobbles, the clanging of a streetcar bell or the familiar cries of men and women selling coal, fruit, and vegetables in Philadelphia.

Suddenly her skipping feet paused. Her eyes were fixed in unbelief on a printed handbill lying on the pavement. That small face down in the corner? Surely that was her own face. She stooped slowly and picked it up. Beneath her picture she read: "Come and hear the baby contralto, ten years old."

She went slowly to the store, the paper clutched in

her hand. Her aunt had planned a concert to help raise a building fund for a small church. Marian had been asked to sing, but had not known that her picture would be printed on a handbill.

The clerk was busy. "Well, now, what would you like?"

"I—I—forget. . . . I guess potatoes."

When she reached her home on Colorado Street she found her mother at the coal range, enveloped by a warm, rich scent of cooking. The two younger girls, Alyce and Ethel, were playing house under the table. Her mother noticed the bag of potatoes.

"Why, Marian, I told you to get me a loaf of bread. Take those potatoes right back."

Marian ran back for the bread, with the handbill held tightly in her hand. She could scarcely wait for her father to come home from his work in the refrigerator room of the Reading Terminal Market. The little sisters squealed with joy at the sight of a pound cake in his hand, but Marian's usual delight in her favorite dessert was dimmed by her excitement. When her father walked in and read the handbill the surprise, soon replaced by pride, in his face was a special gift to her.

Two years before she had sung a duet, "Dear to the Heart of the Shepherd," in church with her friend Viola who lived across the street. This was different. Marian thought the whole world had been told that she was going to sing alone.

As she stood on the stage in the little hall she was so frightened she didn't believe that she could sing. Then she saw the smiling faces of John and Annie Anderson, and beside them Ethel and Alyce leaning forward eagerly, and music poured out. The "baby contralto" gave her first solo performance, and, later,

as the applause died down and the concert ended, she received her first fee. It was fifty cents.

Marian attended church services with her father. Her family was divided in church membership. Her mother was a Methodist, grandmother Anderson went to the Baptist Church, and her grandfather belonged to a Jewish synagogue.

When Marian was ten years old her father had a tragic accident while working and, after months in bed, died of the head injury. Mrs. Anderson, who had been a teacher before she married, could get no work except laundering and cleaning and had to move in with her husband's parents. Marian found grandmother's house a noisy but interesting place, where small children were tended while their mothers went out to work. Grandmother ran her home with a kindly, firm hand. She was proud of the fact that she was part Indian and was always ready to talk about it. Marian took any job that she could do after school and on Saturdays. She delivered laundry, learned to sew, and scrubbed front steps for neighbors for ten cents a job.

Marian studied well in school. Yet the only class that made her happy was music. During her school years she sang in the church choirs, first in the junior choir and then at thirteen in both junior and senior choirs. By the time she entered high school she had already given a performance with a group that put on a show at the Philadelphia Academy of Music. She could not remember a time when she had not believed that she would be a singer. One evening she saw a play given by a group of excellent Negro actors, and she felt that she wanted to be a part of the magical world of the theater. She came to dream of singing and acting in the Metropolitan Opera Company, even though she knew that such a thought was fantastic for her.

Life was busy and exciting enough. Marian was often a soloist in the church choir, and she sometimes substituted for an absent soprano, tenor, or bass. This was an amazing feat, but it developed the astonishing range of her voice. Marian was singing in school concerts also, and since she had a piano at home she tried to learn to play her own accompaniments. As she earned more fees she was able to pay for a few lessons, even though they could not be on a regular basis. Her energetic aunt went with her to engagements at the Y.W.C.A. and Y.M.C.A. and to schools and churches. Marian made very little money, however, for her fees were small and sometimes she was not paid at all. When she grew more confident she began to charge five dollars for an engagement. Two dollars were given to her mother, and one each to her sisters. One dollar she kept for herself.

Then her friends in the church came to her rescue. The pastor took up a collection one Sunday for "our Marian," and the congregation dropped into the plate their hard-earned

nickels and dimes. With this gift of seventeen dollars and two cents Marian bought satin material and gold braid and made a dress herself. She spread her new satin gown over her bed, and stood back to admire it. She had a beautiful dress to wear when she sang, and she wore it to every concert for a long time.

When the tall, slender girl stood on a platform, with her hands clasped simply before her and her wonderful voice filling the hall, who would notice whether she wore a new dress or not? It pleased her to have a satin gown, and yet she was happiest with her knowledge that she could touch drab lives with magic and bring both smiles and tears when she sang.

There wasn't much time for social life, but Marian was young and enjoyed a party when she could go to one. A reception given by a Mr. and Mrs. Fisher in Wilmington, Delaware, turned out to be an important night for Marian Anderson, although she didn't know it at the time.

After a concert in which she had taken part she went

with a friend to the Fisher home. There were two boys in the family who were, like Marian, still in high school and they were both attracted to the shy singer. They found reasons to go to Philadelphia often and always went to see her. For a while she scarcely knew which she liked better, and then the taller brother, Orpheus, who was called King, won out. King Fisher came to art school in Philadelphia, and this gave him an advantage. Nevertheless Marian refused to consider marriage. After a while he left to study architecture in New York, and after that she saw him only occasionally.

The Union Baptist Church remained her favorite place to sing. It was so well known for its music that visitors to Philadelphia often went there, and Reverend Parks, the minister, helped stage a big concert every year, engaging important Negro singers as guest artists. The favorite was Roland Hayes, famous both in Europe and America, and he came many times.

After Marian had appeared on a program with him he congratulated her, and then went to see her grandmother to tell her that Marian should have professional study. Everyone agreed that she should; the question was *how?* Lessons cost money, and Marian's family could not afford it. They did not even know what the fees were at a music school. "Well," said Mrs. Anderson, "it will not harm you to find out."

Marian went to a small music school and waited her turn at the information booth. The girl stared at Marian and then turned to the next person in line. Finally, when she had finished with everyone else, she asked rudely, "What do you want?"

"Will you tell me, please, what it costs to enter. . . ."

"We don't take colored."

100

Marian turned and went slowly homeward. She had not thought much about the problems that her race faced, for her street had both white and Negro families living together without trouble. This was a first real shock, although it was not to be her last.

A friend soon came to help. He introduced her to Mrs. Mary Saunders Patterson, who had a fine soprano voice, and who had studied with a professional teacher. Mrs. Patterson, also a Negro, understood Marian's problems. When she found that her pupil could not pay for lessons she gave them to her free, and when Marian took part in the first concert given by Mrs. Patterson, her teacher presented her with her first real evening dress.

Mrs. Patterson told Marian that she must have an accompanist. As she was considering the matter and wondering what to do about it, a well-known pianist, Billy King, heard her sing and asked to be her accompanist. The number of her engagements increased until she reached a point where singing was interfering with school work. She was able to graduate only because her teachers were sympathetic and gave her make-up work when she missed classes.

After graduation she had more tours. She sang in halls in and around Philadelphia, as well as in colleges and for club programs. Her first trip South provided a second shock. She and her accompanist had to ride in dusty, uncomfortable "Jim Crow" coaches reserved for Negroes only. She could eat at the waiters' table in the diner. Later on, when she made more money, she was permitted to occupy a small room with a door in the sleeping car, if it had not already been sold.

As her income reached higher levels, climbing to fifty dollars a performance and then to a hundred, Marian had the joy of providing a home for her mother and sisters. Mrs. Anderson retired from outside work to live in the small house near Marian's grandmother. It was a great day for Marian when she could take her mother and sisters out to buy furniture for the house. The small home was a modest one, but Mrs. Anderson was there to care for her girls. In bare hotel rooms, as she traveled, Marian dreamed of coming home to the house, filled with affection and music, and always ready to welcome her.

After a year with Mrs. Patterson, Marian Anderson gave a solo concert under the auspices of the Philadelphia Choral Society, and the proceeds provided her with funds to study with Agnes Reifsnyder in Philadelphia. Later friends raised the money for her to become a pupil of Giuseppe Boghetti. Until she was twenty Marian had suffered disappointments in her life many times—but never in the reception given her music. She expected to work hard on her training. Her new teacher, her successful small tours, and her good notices in the newspapers gave her confidence. So she decided to give a concert in Town Hall, in New York City. She prepared for it carefully with Mr. Boghetti, and as she stepped out on the stage to sing she thought that she was ready.

Her heart sank as she faced an auditorium only partly filled. Worst of all, she knew then, as the concert ended, that her knowledge of German and French was imperfect, and that her remarkable natural voice was not yet well trained. As she read the reviews in the papers next day she felt the worst sense of failure of her lifetime. It was some time before her confidence returned, and she could go on again to learning. At least now she knew how much she needed to learn.

Miss Anderson's first contest had been one held by the Philharmonic Society in Philadelphia in 1923. She had taken the winner's certificate. Two years later Mr. Boghetti prepared her to enter a more important contest put on by the Lewisohn Stadium Concerts in New York.

It was summer, and Marian had decided to learn to swim. When she was not studying and practicing singing she went to the Y.W.C.A. to take swimming lessons. This wasn't easy, for it seemed to her that she always sank like a stone in water. Yet, no matter how much water went into her nose, mouth, and ears, she said firmly to herself, "I will learn to swim," and kept on trying.

On that hot day as she waited for her turn to sing for the contest judges in New York she was trying not to worry about a painful infection caused by water in the ear passage. Afterwards, at home again, she felt better and was happy to learn that she was one of sixteen contestants chosen to sing in the finals.

When the day came for the finals she said nothing about her ear, although the pain was worse. After the try-out she was in such acute distress that she sat silently in Mr. Boghetti's New York studio, in fear that she might lose her hearing and be unable to sing again. When the telephone rang and the news came that she had won, all she could murmur was, "I must go home."

She called her doctor at once in Philadelphia. It was only after the pain was relieved by treatment that she began to realize that she had won her big opportunity. Newspapers were acclaiming her, for this contest had drawn the best young singers from across the nation.

On the day that Marian Anderson sang with the New York Philharmonic Orchestra at Lewisohn Stadium the great crowd looked faceless to her—and yet she knew that her family and friends were out there and were with her in spirit. Remembering her disastrous Town Hall concert, she felt a surge of joy at her success.

The appearance with the New York Philharmonic made a change in her life. She soon had a manager, and she sang in larger halls with higher fees. She began to realize that she could no longer sing to Southern audiences where Negroes had to sit in the balcony. She made a desegregated audience a condition of acceptance of invitations.

In her studies with Mr. Boghetti Marian Anderson had made a great deal of progress in foreign languages as well as in her music training. Yet she knew that she must study in Europe to perfect the German Lieder songs that she wanted to sing well. Her first trip, however, was to England, and she paid for it herself from her small savings. She did not gain as much intensive study as she had hoped, but the winter abroad took away some of her shyness and increased her knowledge of people.

Marian Anderson's second trip to Europe was financed by the Julius Rosenwald Foundation. In Berlin, Germany, she lived with a family where she had to speak only German. She studied German Lieder, poems set to music by great composers, with Michael Raucheisen. One day as she sang in his studio two men came quietly in to listen. They were introduced as Rule Rasmussen, a Norwegian concert manager, and Kosti Vehanen, a Finnish pianist. The manager asked Miss Anderson to give a concert tour of the Scandinavian countries, with Vehanen as accompanist.

The first concert, in Oslo, Norway, was a musical sensation. The contralto was almost overwhelmed with praise, with flowers, with good notices, with calls, and with invitations for more concerts. After that exciting tour she went to Finland, where she met the famous composer, Jan Sibelius. On later tours she gave concerts in Russia and in Austria. The newspapers wrote that her appearances left an epidemic of "Marian Fever" behind them.

It was in Austria that Miss Anderson was most moved

by her reception, for there she met Maestro Arturo Toscanini, the greatest orchestra conductor of his day. She felt so honored to be shaking his hand that it was only afterward that she was fully aware of his words. "Yours is a voice such as one hears once in a hundred years."

In Paris she met Mr. Sol Hurok, the impresario who became her manager. Kosti Vehanen came to the United States with her as her accompanist. They found a room with a piano on shipboard to practice for a Town Hall concert. This second appearance at Town Hall in New York City was important to her for she well remembered her first one there.

When the ship was on its third day out Marian Anderson, on her way to the rehearsal room, lost her footing and fell down a companionway stair. Her ankle hurt, but she decided to ignore it. She sang for the ship's concert and on arrival in New York walked ashore. The following day her ankle was badly swollen, and she was told that the bone was cracked. How was she to appear at Town Hall with her ankle in a cast? How could she sing on crutches? How could she get on and off the stage? She was desperately unhappy about it.

In New York, with a nurse standing by, Miss Anderson made plans with her manager. She refused to tell the public she had a broken ankle. When the audience arrived at the hall they saw a closed curtain, which rose to reveal the contralto standing by the piano. She was dressed in a long black and gold brocade grown. When the concert was over, she stood there to prolonged applause as the curtain came down. Her return to Town Hall was a triumph.

In 1939 Mr. Hurok booked an engagement for her in

Constitution Hall, Washington, D. C. She was famous throughout the world now. In the United States Marian Anderson had sung in Carnegie Hall and other large auditoriums. Although newspapers announced that the Daughters of the American Revolution, the organization owning the hall, had refused to permit a Negro to sing there, Marian Anderson paid little attention to the rising storm. She was concerned about the illness of Kosti Vehanen. Her new accompanist was Franz Rupp, who soon became a good friend also. It was only when she arrived in Washington that she began to realize how much of a hurricane the refusal of the hall had raised.

The country took sides in the controversy. Mrs. Eleanor Roosevelt resigned from the D.A.R. Other resignations and protests poured in, and some came from the South. Whole groups in the D.A.R. protested. Although Marian Anderson was not a fighting type of person, and she had no anger or bitterness toward anyone, the simple facts put her in the front of the fight for freedom for all artists, and especially for those of her race.

On Easter Sunday of that year Marian Anderson was unhappy. She felt only sorrow for the women who had raised this issue, and she thought that they simply could not understand. She was never willing to believe that they wished to persecute her as a person. Yet that Easter Sunday was a most difficult day for her. It had been necessary to accept the invitation of the Secretary of the Interior, Mr. Harold L. Ickes, to sing in the open before the Lincoln Memorial instead of in Constitution Hall.

Standing in front of the tall, seated statue of Abraham Lincoln, Marian Anderson was surrounded by famous people, including members of the Congress, some of whom were Southerners.

It comforted her to know that, among the exalted, her mother was quietly near her, praying silently, to help her gain strength. A vast audience of 75,000 people was waiting along the pools facing the Memorial.

She first sang "The Star Spangled Banner" and then other songs, including three Negro spirituals. She was so moved that she did not know whether she sang well or not. She only knew that she sang for all peoples, of all races and religions. Although she had not chosen to be a central figure in a battle for freedom and brotherhood, somehow that was what she was. Marian Anderson was singing for the right to sing, in a country with a constitution built on freedom.

This concert led to Constitution Hall later, where Miss Anderson sang for a benefit, and then later in a concert of her own.

During her years of study and her concert tours Marian Anderson had not forgotten Orpheus Fisher, who had become an

108

architect in New York. They were married in 1943, and her husband designed and built a home for her near Danbury, Connecticut. Marian Anderson is a great lady of the world, but she still finds it impossible to stay afloat in the Fisher swimming pool. She knows that there are just some things that not everybody can do.

Miss Anderson has received so many honors that it is impossible to list them. Among these are many awards, honorary degrees, and medals, including one from the King of Sweden and another from the Emperor of Japan. She has received decorations from Finland, France, Liberia, and other countries, as well as towns and cities throughout the world.

In 1957 Miss Anderson toured India and the Far East for the State Department, and a memorable film was made of her journey. She was hailed everywhere as "America's Good Will Ambassador." She sang at the inaugurations of both President Dwight D. Eisenhower and President John F. Kennedy, and she has given concerts for servicemen in lonely, distant places. Her records delight music lovers in their homes, and her television appearances are special events. Marian Anderson has given generously of her time and interest to underprivileged children in Harlem and to struggling music students.

President Eisenhower appointed Miss Anderson a delegate to the United Nations in 1958, and she has served there with distinction.

In 1954 a dream came true for Marian Anderson. She sang in the Metropolitan Opera House in New York, as Ulrica in Verdi's "Masked Ball." She was the first member of her race to do so. In 1958 Marian Anderson's autobiography was published by the Viking Press. Its title is MY LORD, WHAT A MORNING. It is dedicated to her mother.

The road had been long and difficult since a small girl had paused to stare, unbelievingly, at a handbill on the sidewalk and recognized her own face. As the glorious voice of Marian Anderson catches the hearts of her listeners of other nations it does not matter that sometimes some of them cannot understand her English words. Her spiritual quality reaches them with the beauty of her music. Marian Anderson has never felt alone. She is always conscious of the family, friends, and well-wishers who have helped her and who are with her. And she is deeply religious. She has said that the Bible is the book that has influenced her most throughout her life.

"He's got the wind and the rain in His hands. He's got you and me, brother, in His hands. He's got you and me, sister, in His hands. He's got everybody here in His hands. He's got the whole world in His hands."

110

A Game Called "X"

ALBERT EINSTEIN

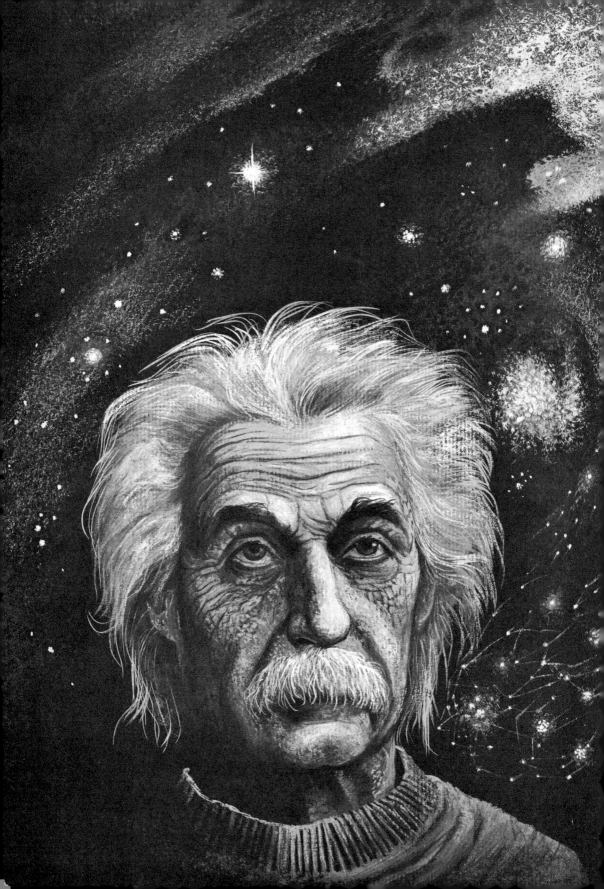

In the eighteen-eighties the old City of Munich, Germany, on the River Isar, still looked like the Middle Ages. A new city was spreading around it, however, encircling the old streets, the ancient cathedral, and the fourteenth-century town hall. Art galleries and museums, scientific exhibits, and the university made this city the center of Bavaria. People from everywhere came there to buy bronze, glass, wood carvings, and the finest astronomical instruments in the world. Munich was an exciting place for a boy to grow up in. It was the city of Albert Einstein's childhood.

Albert was small for his age and very quiet. He spent much more of his life at home than in the old streets, for he seemed to catch every illness that was going around. He was often in a big bed all day, lying under a feather cover that puffed up in his face until only his shock of black curly hair and his enormous dark eyes were visible. On such an evening, when Albert was five years old, his father came in from his electrochemical factory and opened the door of his son's room. Albert smiled, but did not speak.

"I have brought you a little present." Hermann Einstein held out a compass. "Do you see this tiny needle? No matter how you turn it the needle always points to the north."

Albert gazed in wonder at the small object in his hand, turning and moving it to watch that magic needle. He murmured his thanks to his father and kept his wonder to himself. The compass became his most treasured possession. When it was not in his hand it was usually in his pocket.

Albert Einstein had been born in Ulm in 1879. Ulm was in a part of Bavaria called Swabia, not far from Munich, to which the Einstein family moved when Albert was a year old. Bavarians were friendly, easy-going people, not much like the more militaristic Prussians of north Germany. In 1879 Germany was a new nation. It was the result of a joining of ancient kingdoms after a war with France. Royal families still ruled many of these small states. Although the new Germany was governed by Prussia, from its capitol in Berlin, Bavaria was the most independent state within the nation. King Ludwig II was the ruler.

The Einstein household was comfortable and happy. Maja, two years younger than her brother, seemed a normal bright child, but Herr Einstein and his wife were a bit anxious about their son. Albert spoke so seldom that they feared he was slightly retarded in intelligence. They were surprised and delighted to see that he liked the little compass so much and played with it so intently.

To Albert, however, the compass was not something to play with. He did not look on it as a toy, as they supposed, but as something to ask questions about in his own thoughts. He kept these thoughts to himself. His chief pleasures were the evenings in the drawing room when his mother played the piano and her husband sang with her. Observing his love for those musical

114

evenings, they gave Albert a violin so that he could join in the family concerts. Next to his music and his compass, Albert liked most the long, quiet walks that he took with his father through the forests and into nearby mountains.

As Albert grew older his parents realized that, in spite of his slow speech, his mind was not retarded and that they must decide on a school for him. Since they did not believe in the strict orthodox Jewish faith of their own families, their only object was to choose the school where their son could get the best education.

Albert was sent to a Catholic school in Munich. Neither the Jesuit fathers nor the students showed any prejudice against him because of his religion, and yet, since he was the only Jew in the school, he could not feel that he really belonged. Then too the military discipline of a German school of that time was unpleasant for him. He did not learn as much in his classes, where he found Greek and Latin especially difficult, as his parents had hoped. The principal thing he learned was an intense hatred for routine and strict discipline.

One day Uncle Jake came in from his brother's factory, where he worked, with a small book in his hand. Albert's eyes always brightened when he saw Uncle Jake, who was jolly as well as kind.

"This is an algebra book, Albert, and it is full of puzzles. In algebra you can be a hunter, stalking a game called "X." X stands for something unknown. That's exciting, you know. You can pursue that X until you catch it to find out what it is and why and how."

Albert became a great hunter from that day. He stalked his game so often that after a while he found to his surprise that he could catch up with X by ways he figured out for himself, as well as by those given in the textbook. He added mathematics to his love of his compass, music, and walks in the forest. He was lonely much of the time, without friends of his own age. On his rambles along streams and through fields and woods he moved in his own thoughts as completely as if he had taken up a life on the moon. When he returned to the world around him he really felt as if he had come to earth from some distant planet. Although his parents were more encouraged about him and knew that he was not backward, they found it hard to understand him. His mind moved away from them so completely at times that he did not hear or even see things around him.

Then, Max Talmey, a medical student, became his friend. The Einsteins, in spite of their lack of belief in ancient religious observances, lived with the best traditions of their faith. One of these was the practice of inviting a poor Jewish student to dinner once a week.

Max gave Albert a book on geometry. When Albert,

who was then ten years old, opened this book he felt, even more than with algebra, as if he had opened a door and walked right into a bright new world—a world in which he was at home. He read the book through, and then he read it over and over. In the clear, logical propositions of geometry he saw, for the first time, order in the whole universe. To him order was beauty. The universe had its own laws, he knew, if only man could find them. This book made him feel so excited that he could scarcely wait to go into a geometry class which had just been opened in his school.

His teacher never forgot the first day in that class! Albert, the silent, backward boy, revealed an understanding of geometry that went far beyond the textbook. The teacher asked him to wait after school. In a bewildered, angry tone he said, "Albert, will you please do me the favor not to ask me any more questions in class? As a personal favor, do not ask questions."

Albert nodded and then went for a walk, taking the longest way home, to think this out. He knew more than his teacher did—on the first day in geometry class! That was plain to him. So he would have to try to find his own answers.

Five years later Max Talmey completed his medical training and went to New York to practice. Hermann Einstein's factory was not making money, and he was facing bankruptcy. Albert's father decided to take his wife and daughter to Italy, where he had heard that conditions were more promising for his kind of work. Albert, he thought, should not go, for he was still in school. He arranged board and room for his son in a friend's home.

Albert was quite alone now. He was fifteen and he talked well, when he wished. He had made a few casual friends, but he was not doing any better in school. He believed that wars and armies and the use of force were wrong, and he often failed to follow the military rules on which school discipline was based. He just ignored them. One day the head of the school called him to his office.

"Albert, we have decided that you can no longer study here."

"I haven't caused any trouble, have I?"

"No, but your attitude toward discipline is a bad example for the other boys."

For a long time Albert had wanted to leave the school, and now he did it. He gathered up his clothing and went to join his family in Milan. When he arrived, his parents rejoiced. They had received word from the school that he had left and they had

been very worried. Albert was happy to play his violin with his family in the evenings and to spend his days wandering about the exciting Italian city. He put off plans for his future.

Then his father failed in business again, and Albert could no longer expect help from him. Albert wanted to be a mathematician, but since he had no diploma from his German school, further study seemed impossible. Then relatives—aunts, uncles, and cousins—together arranged a small monthly sum for him. He left for Switzerland with the hope of attending school there.

Einstein arrived at the Swiss Polytechnical School in Zürich. In spite of the astonishing knowledge that he showed in mathematics, he was denied admittance.

"Go to a cantonal school," advised the director, "and learn languages. There is a good one in Aarau."

Albert's spirits were low as he traveled to Aarau. When he arrived, however, he was surprised to find that the school welcomed him. There were no military rules. Everyone was friendly.

One of the teachers took him home to board with his family. This year in Aarau was one of the happiest of his life, and he made a good record in his studies.

Returning to the Polytechnical School in Zürich as an assistant science teacher the following year, Albert Einstein discovered that physics seemed to offer more opportunity to find the answers to his questions about the forces that move the universe than did mathematics. His first sense of wonder as he had looked at the little needle on the compass so long ago had not left him. It had grown into a compelling passion to understand the beauty and order of natural laws. He gave up his German citizenship and became a citizen of Switzerland. His relatives could not help him much, and he had to spend every moment away from the school working at various jobs to earn money for his needs. Yet it was during this strenuous time that he got his Ph.D. degree. His health suffered from the life he led, for he was often hungry.

The great wealth of scientific books available to him was like a treasure, and he made good use of them. There were a few friends, also, who had the same kind of interests. One was a young Hungarian girl, Mileva Maritsch, from a Greek Orthodox Catholic family. Like Albert, she was planning to teach physics. Albert's love for music was as compelling as ever. These two saved a few francs whenever they could and spent them on cheap seats high in the balcony of the opera house.

As soon as he had received his Ph.D., Einstein began looking for a full teaching position. His high hopes were soon dashed, for none was available to him. He wanted to marry Mileva, and without a position that was impossible. So Albert Einstein took a place as a clerk in the Swiss Patent Office in Bern. During the first few years of his marriage those who knew him saw only a rather silent, hard-working young man with a wife and two small boys.

Not even his closest friends knew that Einstein, since the age of sixteen, had been evolving some new theories of space and time and the forces that hold the universe together. Until he had completed his college work he could do little to develop the proof of his theories.

Working in the Patent Office required only a very small part of his thought. There was no monotony in the job, for he met inventors and studied their inventions. In fact, he even worked out a few inventions himself in those years. Yet subjects such as the mysteries of light and gravitation absorbed his mind. While he was still in his twenties Albert Einstein was discovering new factors in the relation between matter and energy that seemed to change the basic concepts of the whole world of physics.

By the time he was twenty-six years old Einstein had thought out his theory of relativity, as well as his theory of light. At home when he retreated into his own thoughts and closed the door, in that remarkable concentration that was part of his genius, not even his wife could enter. He was always fond of his sons, but the years drew Mileva and Albert so far apart that they realized their marriage was failing.

From 1901 to 1905 Dr. Einstein published scientific papers in a German magazine called *The Year Book of Physics.* One of them developed his theories on light, and the principle evolved by him led inventors later on to produce television and make other uses of the photoelectric cell.

His fourth published paper dealt with space and time,

presenting what soon became known as Einstein's Theory of Relativity. It took the scientific world a while to realize that here was the work of one of the greatest geniuses of all time—that here was a theory that would change our whole understanding of the universe. A few scientists grasped this immediately, but for the most part its implications were ignored. The theory itself was so complicated, and its mathematical proof so difficult, that even today there are only a few who can fully master it.

After Dr. Einstein completed his first formulation of these theories and finished his scientific papers, he had a physical and nervous collapse and was ill for several weeks.

"I lived through a superhuman mental effort that was so intense it was like a blinding light," he said.

Nevertheless, as soon as he recovered he began again to re-examine other theories of physics and of mechanical laws as they were then known to scientists. He published another study that added knowledge to his first papers. This established the scientific basis for breaking the atom, releasing for the first time unlimited energy and power for man's use. This paper produced no more excitement in the scientific world than had the first ones.

Dr. Einstein accepted a teaching post in the University of Zürich, and in 1910 he transferred to the university in Prague, Czechoslavakia.

There he was asked to indicate his religion. This information was requested on a routine form. A friend said, "Don't put down Jewish. Better leave the space blank." Einstein did not reply. Instead he wrote, "Israelite." He had never before thought in terms of Jew or Gentile.

It was in Prague that he was first made acutely aware of

122

widespread discrimination against Jews in the social life of the university. His indifference to social convention and his preference for old clothes, long solitary walks, and the company of his violin, did not help his reputation with faculty wives.

By 1913 important scientists were recognizing the genius of this quiet, modest man. He was invited to become a member of the Kaiser Wilhelm Institute, and a teaching post was created especially for him in the Prussian Academy of Science in Berlin. This was a great honor, one extended only to the most distinguished scientists. He was also asked to resume his German citizenship, and when he refused they agreed to take him without it.

The move to Berlin brought Albert and Mileva to a parting for life. They were divorced soon after Dr. Einstein moved to Germany. Leaving his boys in Switzerland hurt their father, although he saw them as often as he could.

When he came to Berlin Professor Einstein felt that he was fortunate to have relatives there who wanted him to make his home with them. He lived with a cousin whose widowed daughter, Elsa, kept house for him. Albert, who had been always a shy, lonely man, now found a happy companionship with Elsa, her father, and her two little girls.

The year after he returned to Germany was 1914, and the peace of Europe was shattered by the eruption of the first world war. Professor Einstein was strongly opposed to war, and he said so, feeling that he could speak freely since he was not a German citizen. Yet four years later, when the war had ended, he yielded to the persuasion of friends who told him that it would help the new German republic to have the world-famous name of

Einstein on its roll of citizens. He took out citizenship papers.

Dr. Einstein, who called himself a "citizen of the world" now, once more became a German citizen. The years that followed were peaceful and promising years for him, in spite of the poverty and unrest of the defeated nation. Elsa became Albert's wife and together they traveled to many countries, where Dr. Einstein lectured to scientists. The public generally did not understand his theories, of course, but people knew that Einstein was a great genius and they respected and admired him. His large head, with the shock of dark hair turning gray above his brilliant eyes, made him stand out in any group. He was recognized everywhere.

124

He and Elsa and the girls lived in a village outside
Berlin, where the professor could sail his boat on a nearby lake
and go for his beloved long walks whenever he wished.

Conditions in Germany were growing worse. Each time
the Einsteins returned from abroad they noticed changes that were
ominous. After Adolf Hitler and the Nazis came to power Elsa
grew frightened at the violent attacks being made more and more
frequently on Jewish people. Even the most distinguished Jews
were in danger. Friends urged the Einsteins to leave Germany.

Dr. Einstein had not forgotten that he had, as early as
1931, been invited to teach at a newly formed scientific institute

for advanced study in Princeton, New Jersey. His position in Germany was dangerous, since he was now a citizen. His work with the Jewish Zionist group, which was trying to found a new state of Israel, added to the danger.

The Einsteins moved to Belgium. Dr. Einstein resigned his professorship and his membership in the Kaiser Wilhelm Institute. They worried about their daughters, who remained in Germany. Persecution and officially approved murder of political prisoners and Jews became one of the great crimes in the history of the world. Dr. Einstein decided to go to America to carry on his work. He and Mrs. Einstein moved to Princeton, New Jersey, to establish their permanent home.

One day in 1939, with World War II just over the horizon, Dr. Einstein received an urgent request from scientific friends who were also in America. They asked him to write President Franklin D. Roosevelt that the noted scientists, Dr. Fermi and Dr. Szilard, believed that uranium could be turned into the most powerful source of energy in world history. A nuclear bomb could destroy a whole city. They were convinced that in Germany experiments of this kind were about to produce such a bomb. It was strongly felt that such a project should be started in America without delay.

Dr. Einstein quickly sent the letter. Impressed by the scientific authority behind this recommendation, President Roosevelt agreed. The first, or Manhattan Project, was begun. Carried on with the greatest secrecy during the early years of the war, the program reached its goal with the world's first atomic explosion over the New Mexico desert on the morning of July 16, 1945.

After the atomic bombs were dropped on Japan in 1945

Dr. Einstein was profoundly concerned about the great destruction of human life. He issued a statement in which he wrote that had he known that Germany was not as near success as had been believed by scientists outside that country he would not have written his famous letter. It was his own theory of the relation between mass and energy that had so changed scientific thought that the development of the atomic bomb was possible.

For the rest of his life Dr. Einstein wrote and worked in every way he could to try to make people understand that this new force could destroy almost all life on the earth. So little was known about the effects of radiation and atomic fallout that, even without war, just from the results of test explosions, the human race could be seriously damaged.

After the war Dr. Einstein lived quietly with his wife and one of her daughters in Princeton. Later, after Elsa died, his sister Maja came to join his household. In the evenings the sound of his violin could be heard by his neighbors along the tree-lined street.

The greatest genius since Galileo and Newton could be seen walking slowly down the street, in his comfortable old sweater, baggy trousers, and sandals. His white hair stood out untidily around his large head, but his dark eyes were as brilliant and thoughtful as in the days when he tramped the Bavarian mountain trails. Princeton children all knew Dr. Einstein. He stopped often to speak to them. They all knew, too, that Dr. Einstein had received the Nobel prize and that from all over the world important people came to see him.

He was unassuming and kindly, and he never quite understood why the world should treat him as a great man. Albert Einstein's goal was not his own gain, or even his own happiness. He said that he believed in goodness, beauty, and truth and that these were part of the natural laws of the universe.

When Albert Einstein died in 1954 the world lost a man who was not only an all-time genius, but also a great human being.